MW00559124

TRACK PLANS FOR
Lionel
FasTrack

KB
KALMBACH BOOKS

Kalmbach Books
21027 Crossroads Circle
Waukesha, Wisconsin 53186
www.Kalmbach.com/Books

© 2013 Kalmbach Books
All rights reserved. This book may not be reproduced in part or in whole by any means whether electronic or otherwise without written permission of the publisher except for brief excerpts for review.

Published in 2013
27 26 25 24 23   6 7 8 9

Manufactured in the United States of America

ISBN: 978-0-89024-966-6

Editor: Randy Rehberg
Designer: Patti L. Keipe
Illustrator: Kellie Jaeger
Photographers: William Zuback, Jim Forbes, CTT staff

Lionel® and FasTrack® are registered trademarks of Lionel LLC, Chesterfield, Michigan.

Publisher's Cataloging-In-Publication Data

Track plans for Lionel FasTrack / [editor: Randy Rehberg ; designer: Patti Keipe ; illustrator: Kellie Jaeger].

 p. : col. ill. ; cm. -- (Classic toy trains books)

Some plans have previously appeared in Classic toy trains magazine.
ISBN: 978-0-89024-966-6

 1. Railroad tracks--Models--Design and construction. 2. Railroads--Models--Design and construction. 3. Lionel Corporation. I. Rehberg, Randy. II. Keipe, Patti. III. Jaeger, Kellie. IV. Title: Classic toy trains.

TF197 .T733 2013
625.1/9

Contents

Introduction

This book contains 25 track plans that were specially designed for use with Lionel FasTrack. Most of them have appeared in *Classic Toy Trains* magazine, but some have been expanded upon for this book, and several were newly created. The majority fall into the manageable small to midsize range, with a few more ambitious room-size layouts thrown in. They include a variety of themes from Christmas to logging to the Wild West.

A description of the layout, a list of needed FasTrack components, and operating tips accompany each track plan. Some plans also include suggested accessories and scenery ideas. In addition to the track plans, the book provides some handy information on converting traditional O gauge layouts to FasTrack.

FasTrack components

Introduced in 2003, FasTrack components have become a popular alternative to traditional tubular track. Similar to traditional tubular track, FasTrack curved and straight track sections are available in a variety of sizes (see page 7 for a comparison of the two types). Specialty items include uncoupling, operating, railer, and accessory-activator sections. Accessories feature various grade crossings, bumper sections, and crossovers.

While FasTrack components are more expensive than traditional tubular track, they are easy to use and provide a reliable electrical connection (see page 7 for a track cost comparison).

Track component key

Perhaps the greatest benefit of a printed track plan is the guidance it provides when assembling specific track components. The necessary track pieces are listed in a handy color-coded key, such as the one shown at right. Quantities and the product number for each section are also included.

Straight track is shown as squares, curves as circles, and track switches (turnouts) as triangles. Unique colors and symbols within these shapes identify special track sections. On the track plan, these shapes show the precise placement for each section of track.

Whether you are converting a layout to FasTrack or planning a new one, the track plans in this book should provide you with necessary tools and inspiration to create your own exciting O gauge layout.

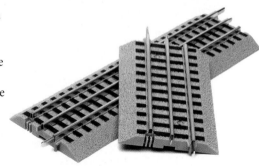

Track component key

LIONEL FASTRACK COMPONENTS	
Quantity	Description/Number
2	1.75-inch straight (12026)
1	4.5-inch straight (12025)
2	5-inch straight (12024)
5	10-inch straight (12014)
6	O-36 curve, 11.25-degree (12023)
1	O-36 curve 22.5-degree (12022)
14	O-36 curve, 45-degree (12015)
2	O-48 curve, 30-degree (12043)
1	O-36 left-hand track switch (12017)
2	O-36 right-hand track switch (12018)
1	5-inch uncoupler (12020)
2	bumper (12059)

Adapting a Track Plan

Kids used to be able to create a new toy train layout in the blink of an eye. All they needed were a bundle of tubular track, permission to move a few fixtures around the rumpus room, and just a bit of imagination to spawn an endless number of Carpet Central creations. But as youthful builders matured, many learned to appreciate the conveniences of a prescribed plan.

Prescribed plans offer guidance and inspiration to modelers in their layout construction efforts. And with a dizzying array of available track brands, types, and sizes, it's no wonder that we're a bit more hesitant to simply amass a supply of track and start building or modifying a layout on the fly.

Whether you're considering a published track plan or would rather make your own design, be sure to think about the kind of railroad operation you enjoy most, and what specific type of locomotives and rolling stock you intend to run on your layout.

It can be a daunting task to sit down and design an original track plan. But with the number of track plans out there, it is easy to adapt one or more plans for your layout. As Lionel FasTrack becomes more popular, it is more common to see modelers converting their tubular track to FasTrack.

I found that there are four simple steps in adapting a track plan. Using *Classic Toy Trains'* Readers' Choice Railroad as an example, I'll share these key considerations and provide a brief overview of track-planning terms, tips, and techniques. This should make it easier to embrace that youthful urge to design a layout of your own creation!

Readers' Choice Railroad
The evolution of CTT's Readers' Choice Railroad is a good example of adapting a track plan. It was developed during 2011 based on survey responses by CTT readers.

It was first adapted for a layout using Lionel tubular track from the Blue Creek Ry. (see pages 12–13), and then I later retrofitted the Readers' Choice Railroad track plan to suit Lionel FasTrack components.

I'll confess that when CTT readers requested a 4 x 8-foot layout with a mountain railroad theme, I thought only of the impediments to creating such a scheme. But rather than risk disappointing our

Original Blue Creek FasTrack Plan

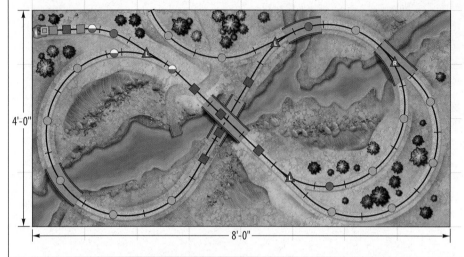

LIONEL FASTRACK COMPONENTS

Quantity	Description/Number
2	1.75-inch straight (12026)
1	4.5-inch straight (12025)
6	10-inch straight (12014)
14	0-36 curve, 45-degree (12015)
3	0-36 curve, 22.5-degree (12022)
3	0-36 curve, 11.25-degree (12023)
3	0-36 left-hand track switch (12045)
1	0-36 right-hand track switch (12046)
1	bumper (12059)

4'-0"
8'-0"

Readers' Choice Traditional Track Plan

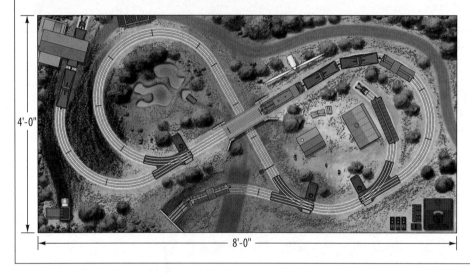

LIONEL O GAUGE TRACK COMPONENTS

Quantity	Description/number
6	10-inch straight
3	custom-cut straight
13	0-31 curve, 45-degree
3	0-31 half-curve, 22.5-degree
2	0-42 curve, 30-degree
1	0-42 custom-cut curve
1	0-31 modern left-hand switch (14062)
2	0-31 modern right-hand switch (14063)
1	uncoupling track (65530)
2	track bumpers (12715)

4'-0"
8'-0"

Readers' Choice FasTrack Plan

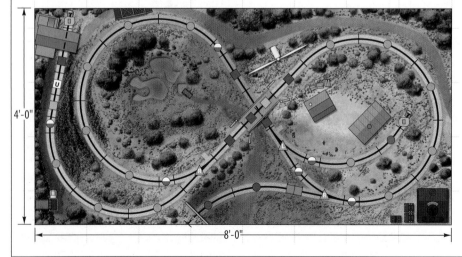

LIONEL FASTRACK COMPONENTS

Quantity	Description/Number
2	1.75-inch straight (12026)
1	4.5-inch straight (12025)
2	5-inch straight (12024)
5	10-inch straight (12014)
6	0-36 curve, 11.25-degree (12023)
1	0-36 curve 22.5-degree (12022)
14	0-36 curve, 45-degree (12015)
2	0-48 curve, 30-degree (12043)
1	0-36 left-hand track switch (12017)
2	0-36 right-hand track switch (12018)
1	5-inch uncoupler (12020)
2	bumper (12059)

4'-0"
8'-0"

Track Types

CURVED TRACK DIAMETERS

	Tubular	FasTrack
O-31	X	X
O-36		X
O-42	X	
O-48		X
O-54	X	
O-60		X
O-72	X	X
O-84		X

TRACK SWITCH DIAMETERS

	Tubular	FasTrack
O-31	X	
O-36		X
O-48		X
O-60		X
O-72	X	X
O-72 wye		X

CROSSINGS

	Tubular	FasTrack
22.5-degree	X	
45-degree	X	X
90-degree	X	X

Track Cost

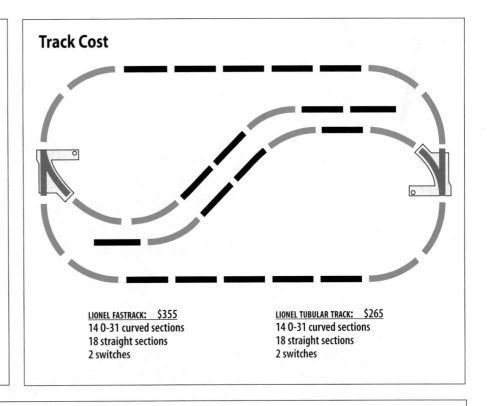

LIONEL FASTRACK: $355
14 0-31 curved sections
18 straight sections
2 switches

LIONEL TUBULAR TRACK: $265
14 0-31 curved sections
18 straight sections
2 switches

Bonus Track Plan

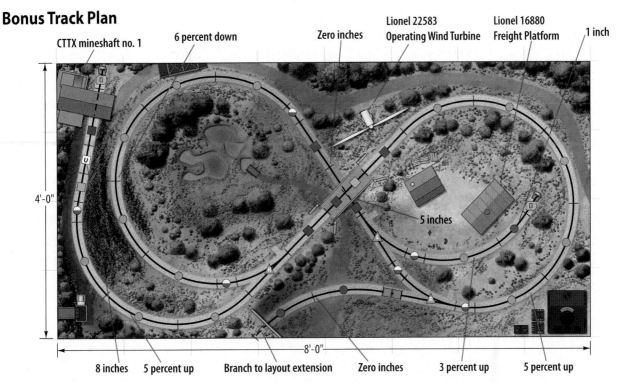

CTTX mineshaft no. 1 — 6 percent down — Zero inches — Lionel 22583 Operating Wind Turbine — Lionel 16880 Freight Platform — 1 inch

4'-0"

5 inches

8 inches — 5 percent up — Branch to layout extension — Zero inches — 3 percent up — 5 percent up

8'-0"

Although not presented in the same format as the other 25 track plans in this book, all the information is here for you to build the Readers' Choice Railroad. The 4 x 8-foot railroad can be a stand-alone layout, or you can combine it with the 3 x 8-foot urban extension, as described on pages 57–59.

As seen in the photo on page 5, the layout was built on prefabricated benchwork topped with ½-inch-thick particleboard. And because the Readers' Choice Railroad requires elevation, a base of 2-inch-thick foam insulation was added.

Then, we used a paper template of the plan to help place the track, accessories, and scenery. A downloadable template is available at ctt.trains.com/operating/how to/2011/05/readers choice template. To use it, print out a full-scale (1" = 1") copy and place the printed sheets on the foam board. Start in one corner, using the grid lines to align the papers. Set down an entire row and tape the sheets to each other and to the foam surface. Once arranged, you can see where the track and accessories go and make any adjustments.

Create Software Sketches

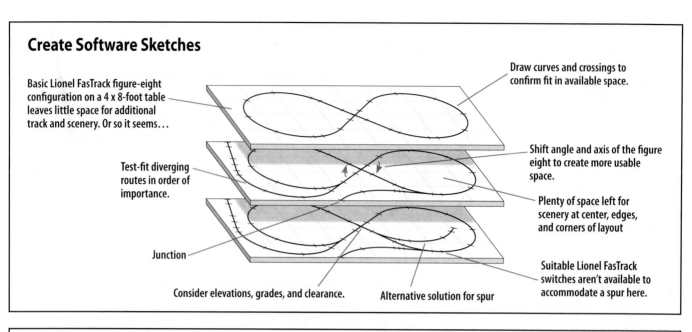

Basic Lionel FasTrack figure-eight configuration on a 4 x 8-foot table leaves little space for additional track and scenery. Or so it seems…

Draw curves and crossings to confirm fit in available space.

Test-fit diverging routes in order of importance.

Shift angle and axis of the figure eight to create more usable space.

Plenty of space left for scenery at center, edges, and corners of layout

Junction

Consider elevations, grades, and clearance.

Alternative solution for spur

Suitable Lionel FasTrack switches aren't available to accommodate a spur here.

Lionel FasTrack Length Table

Track Length	1.375	1.750	4.500	5.000	10.000
1.375	1				
1.750		1			
2.750	2				
3.125	1	1			
3.500		2			
4.125	3				
4.500			1		
4.875	1	2			
5.000				1	
5.250		3			
5.500	4				
5.875	1		1		
6.250		1	1		
6.375	1			1	
6.625	1	3			
6.750		1			
7.000		4			
7.250	2		1		
7.625	1	1	1		
7.750	2			1	
8.000		2	1		
8.125	1	1		1	
8.250	6				
8.375	1	4			
8.500		2		1	
8.625	3		1		
8.750		5			
9.000			2		
9.125	3			1	
9.375	1	2	1		
9.500			1	1	
9.625	7				
9.750		3	1		
9.875	1	2		1	
10.000					1
10.125	1	5			
10.250		3		1	
10.375	1		2		
10.500	4			1	
10.750		1	2		
10.875	1		1	1	
11.000	8				
11.125	1	3	1		
11.250		1	1	1	
11.375	1				1
11.500		4	1		
11.625	1	3		1	
11.750		1			1
11.875	1	6			
12.000		4		1	
12.125	1	1	2		
12.250		7			
12.375	9				
12.500		2	2		
12.625	1	1	1	1	
12.750	2				1
12.875	1	4	1		
13.000		2	1	1	
13.125	1	1			1
13.250		5	1		
13.375	1	4	1		
13.500		2			1
13.625	1	7			
13.750		5	1		
13.875	1	2	2		
14.000		2	1		
14.125	3				1
14.250		3	2		
14.375	1	2	1	1	
14.500		1			1
14.625	1	5	1		
14.750		3	1	1	
14.875	1	2			1
15.000			1	1	
15.125	11				
15.250		3			1
15.375	1		2	1	
15.500	4				1
15.625	1	3	2		
15.750		1	2	1	
15.875	1		1		1
16.000		4	2		
16.125	1	3	1	1	
16.250		1	1		1
16.375	1			1	1
16.500		4	1	1	
16.625	1	3			1
16.750		1		1	1
16.875	5				1
17.000		4			1
17.125	1	1	2	1	
17.250		7		1	
17.375	1	4	2		
17.500		2	2	1	
17.625	1	1	1		1
17.750		5	2		
17.875	3	5	1		
18.000		2	1		1
18.125	1	1		1	1
18.250		5	1	1	
18.375	1	4			1
18.500		2		1	1
18.625	5	1			1
18.750		5			1
18.875	1	2	2	1	
19.000		2			1
19.125	3			1	1
19.250		3	2	1	
19.375	1	2	1		1
19.500			1	1	1
19.625	1	5	1	1	
19.750		1	4		
19.875	1	2		1	1
20.000					2

Compiled by CTT reader Steven Bergerson of Backus, Minn.

readers, I decided to take on the challenge of designing and building a smooth-running compact layout with appreciable elevation and, consequently, significant grades.

In confronting the challenge, I recognized that maintaining a typical 4 to 6 percent rise within the confines of a 4 x 8 footprint was possible only with a grade that began on a straight section of O gauge track and continued through O gauge curves. And that's when I thought back to Blue Creek Ry., a track plan I developed as a permutation of a simple figure-eight scheme.

The Blue Creek track plan features Lionel FasTrack and a 4 percent grade to an overpass I used to replace a limiting 90-degree crossing that's commonly associated with figure-eight schemes. But even better, this plan includes elevations and terrain features that suggest Appalachian coal country.

With a few adaptations and additions to the Blue Creek Ry., I created a new Lionel O gauge track plan for the Readers' Choice Railroad using tubular track. Then, again at readers' requests, I converted the Readers' Choice track plan to one that used FasTrack components. If you look over the three plans on page 6, you can see how the layouts changed and evolved.

Four simple steps

While converting a track plan from tubular track to FasTrack, as I did with the Readers' Choice Railroad, there are four steps you should look at:
- Check for similar plans
- Compare track types
- Consider curves and crossovers
- Create software sketches

CHECK FOR SIMILAR PLANS
Converting a plan isn't an impossible task, but it does take time. Before I go through the effort to convert a scheme, I spend a few moments searching for a plan with characteristics similar to the one I want to convert.

One source for finding alternative track plans is CTT's track plan database. Magazine subscribers visiting ClassicToyTrains.com can easily search more than 100 plans based on layout size, track type, and minimum curve size.

COMPARE TRACK TYPES
You'd think that track products sold by the same manufacturer would be interchange-

Consider the Curves

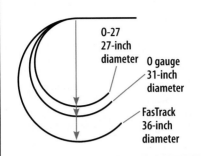

able, right? Not always. Before you decide whether to convert a plan to your preferred track type, be sure to explore just how many sections have complementary parts—especially the curves, switches, and crossings. As the chart comparing Lionel FasTrack and tubular track illustrates (on page 7), only five sizes match. Essentially, fewer matching pieces equates to more challenges in the conversion process.

In addition to knowing what's available in a product line, you'll want to compare the cost of the two brands. The appearance of contemporary track such as FasTrack is remarkable, but it comes at a greater price than 60-year-old tubular rails.

Track cost comparison. Using a simple O gauge track plan consisting of 32 pieces of track and two O-31 remote switches (O-36 in the case of FasTrack), you can get an idea of how the cost of FasTrack compares to traditional tubular track (see page 7). The costs are based on Lionel 2013 catalog prices, although if you shop around online, you can get new FasTrack for about $100 less, and it is even less expensive if you purchase used track.

CONSIDER CURVES AND CROSSOVERS
After comparing two track systems, I look closely at the shape of the original plan to determine how larger and smaller sections affect the overall design. First, I'll focus on one specific loop or route and examine how swapping out curves may alter the length and width of the scheme. Even a seemingly slight change in the geometry of a curve can have a drastic impact on what fits into a prescribed space. Next, I perform a similar survey of the track switches. I pay particular attention to crossovers, where changes in track geometry can expand or constrict the spacing between parallel routes.

5 Track-Planning Tips

These design factors can help you develop a more satisfying track plan.

1 Room to grow
Look for areas on the layout where you can either continue the main line or extend a yard or spur to include new destinations for your trains.

2 More places to play
Adding an operating accessory enhances the play value of a layout—even when the trains aren't running!

3 Mystery and intrigue
A continuous loop of track keeps trains in constant motion, but hills, tunnels, overpasses, and crossings help break up the monotony.

4 Easy to reach
It's best to keep tracks within arm's reach. On larger layouts, it's tempting to bend this rule, but it's never worth the agony in the long run.

5 Park, pass, and run
Look for plans that have a provision for operating a train around one that's parked—either a yard or siding will do.

CREATE SOFTWARE SKETCHES
Once I've gathered these critical insights, it's time to start slogging through a conversion. You may think that a no. 2 pencil and graph paper are the best tools for track planning, but I prefer layout-planning software. RR-Track from R&S Enterprises (rrtrack.com) is my favorite application, as it maintains the widest variety of track libraries from which to choose. Software makes it much easier to virtually test-fit sections of track and avoid the inaccuracies that can occur when drafting with pencil and paper.

Along with software, I find it helps to keep a FasTrack Length Table as a ready reference (on opposite page). The data found in the table makes it a very useful layout design tool. This table gives you a way to determine which combinations of straight track sections can be used to fill a specific length (in inches). Simply measure the length of a desired straight run and reference the table to determine how many of each section you'll need to purchase.

Snaking Curves

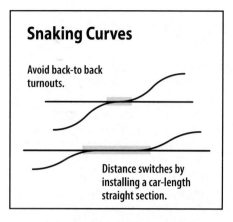

Avoid back-to back turnouts.

Distance switches by installing a car-length straight section.

Track Spacing

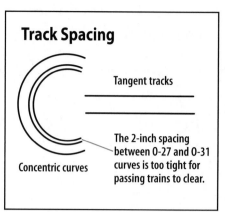

Tangent tracks

Concentric curves

The 2-inch spacing between 0-27 and 0-31 curves is too tight for passing trains to clear.

Maximum Grade and Minimum Clearance

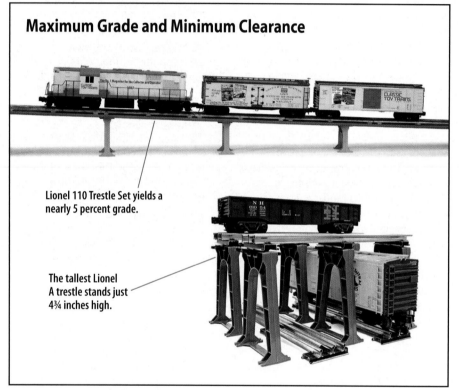

Lionel 110 Trestle Set yields a nearly 5 percent grade.

The tallest Lionel A trestle stands just 4¾ inches high.

Hidden Trackwork

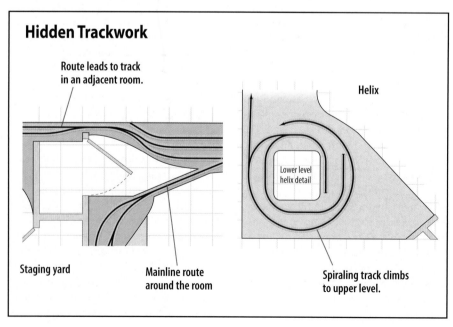

Route leads to track in an adjacent room.

Helix

Lower level helix detail

Staging yard

Mainline route around the room

Spiraling track climbs to upper level.

Track-planning terms

This illustrated glossary presents some basic track-planning terms that will help you better appreciate the intricacies of track planning.

CROSSOVER AND CROSSING

Crossover. Two track switches and a connecting track that allow a train to divert to a parallel track.

Crossing. A track section that allows one route to bisect another. The most common toy train crossings have 45- and 90-degree angles.

TRACK SWITCH AND TURNOUT

Track switch. A section of track featuring movable rails that allows a train to travel from one path to another. A number, such as O-72 or no. 5, designates the curve or angle of the diverting path.

Turnout. A model railroading term that distinguishes a track section from an electrical switch.

SPUR AND SIDING

Stub-end spur. Track section that dead-ends after diverging from the main route.

Passing siding. This section of track also diverges from the main route but later reconnects through a second track switch. A passing siding is typically long enough to hold an entire train while another train travels through the main route.

JUNCTION AND TERMINAL

Junction. A point on a layout where two or more routes meet. Some junctions represent nothing more than the joining of two tracks; others include a complex network of track switches and sidings.

Stub-end terminal. Literally, the ending or starting point of a railroad route. Terminal points exist for freight and passenger trains as well as locomotives.

REVERSE LOOP AND WYE

Reverse loop. A single switch and balloon-shaped track arrangement used to reverse the direction of a train.

Wye. A triangular arrangement of track made of three legs, one of which may be the main route. This track arrangement can be used to change the direction of a locomotive or an entire train.

SNAKING CURVES

S curve. Track arrangements where cars passing from one curve to another are forced to bend in opposite directions. To

Layout Designs

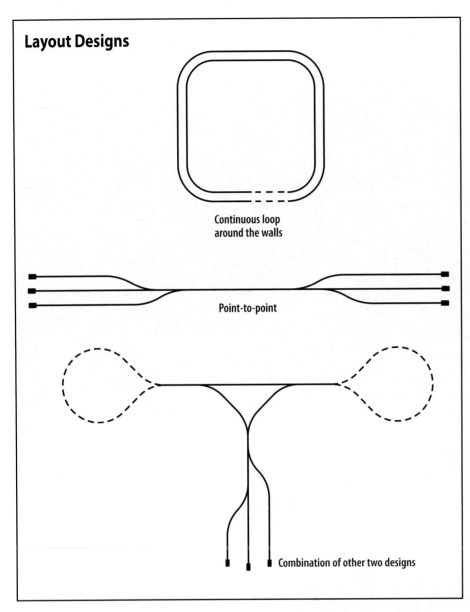

Continuous loop around the walls

Point-to-point

Combination of other two designs

Crossover and Crossing

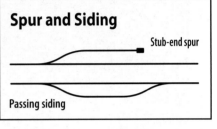

Crossover

Crossing

Spur and Siding

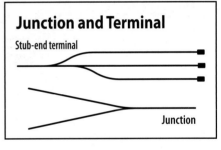

Stub-end spur

Passing siding

Junction and Terminal

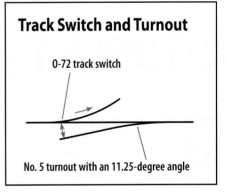

Stub-end terminal

Junction

Track Switch and Turnout

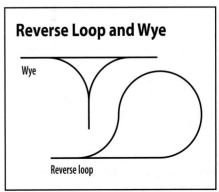

0-72 track switch

No. 5 turnout with an 11.25-degree angle

Reverse Loop and Wye

Wye

Reverse loop

---

prevent derailments, avoid using this arrangement anywhere on a layout.

TRACK SPACING

Tangent tracks. Common spacing for parallel O gauge straight track is 4 inches, center-to-center (distance between the two middle rails).

Concentric curves. A center-to-center spacing of 5½ inches on tight-radius curves provides adequate clearance for most equipment. Using wide-radius curves helps attain a more realistic 4-inch spacing.

MAXIMUM GRADE AND MINIMUM CLEARANCE

Grades. A grade greater than 5 percent (a 5-inch rise over a 100-inch run) presents a challenge to operation. For more reliable running, keep the grade to 4 percent or less.

Clearance. Small O gauge trains can pass under postwar bridges, portals, and trestle sets with a low 4½-inch clearance height (from railhead). However, tall modern toy trains may require an additional inch or more of clearance height.

HIDDEN TRACKWORK

Staging yard. An out-of-sight area used to hold complete trains before running them over visible portion of a layout.

Helix. A rising curve that turns around an axis like a corkscrew. Used on multi-level layouts to allow trains to go from one level to another.

LAYOUT DESIGNS

There are essentially three basic layout designs: continuous, point-to-point, and a combination of these two. All can have provisions for a train to change direction, pass another train, and position cars on sidings.

By Kent Johnson

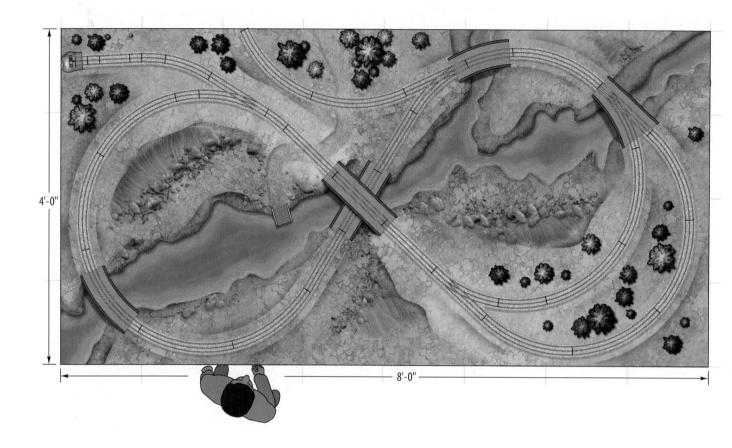

4'-0"

8'-0"

Blue Creek Ry.

Believe it our not, it's not uncommon for aspiring toy train layout builders to request plans for a 4 x 8-foot layout with—get this—a mountain railroad theme. Maybe it's just me, but a 32-square-foot area doesn't immediately conjure up images of trains rolling up and over towering peaks! Nevertheless, I'm not one to back away from a track planning challenge. Even knowing that operating toy trains on grades can be tricky, I still decided to take on the task of designing and building a smooth-running compact layout with appreciable elevation and, consequently, significant grades.

In confronting the challenge, I recognized that maintaining a typical 4–6 percent rise within the confines of a 4 x 8 footprint

was possible only with a grade that began on a 10-inch straight section of Lionel FasTrack and continued through standard O-36 curves. And that's when I remembered the simplicity of a figure-eight scheme.

For starters, I composed a 4 x 8-foot plan that has the initial appearance of a simple figure-eight scheme. But if you look closer, you'll see that the Blue Creek Ry. features an overpass rather than a 90-degree crossing section that limits the length of your trains. Implementing this overpass requires a 4 percent grade, but this made it even easier to include elevations and terrain features that are typical of mountainous regions in the eastern United States.

Making mountains

With the addition of elevation and a few other design features, what was once a simple figure-eight scheme now becomes a functional mountain railroad. At the top of the elevation (approximately 10 inches), you'll find a short siding that doubles as an escape track for runaway locomotives and a place to spot maintenance-of-way cars and motorized vehicles. For true empire builders, this siding could someday lead to an upper mountain branch line expansion beyond the existing 4 x 8 footprint.

Working downgrade, trains roll over a short bridge, around the curve, down to zero elevation, and finally toward a spur that's also positioned with expansion in mind. An up-and-down cycle can be

This short industrial spur also provides means for point-to-point operation to the spur situated below. With the addition of a command control system, you can even consider two-train operation.

Room to expand this railroad comes by way of a spur that runs to the edge of the layout. If you have space in the corner of a room, you can easily form an L-shaped pike by adding another 4 x 8-foot board.

Scenery and structures for the railroad should fit the mountain railroad theme dictated by the tight-radius curves and changing elevations. Also consider using smaller Plasticville structures to make the most of the limited space.

Lionel FasTrack 0-36 curves form the majority of the layout, so it seems logical to develop a layout theme and scenery where sharp curves are expected—a rustic setting in the hills or a busy mine operation are two fitting choices.

A 4 percent grade routes trains up, down, and around the curves at each end of the layout. Don't have a computer or slide rule handy to calculate the proper track elevations? Simply use Woodland Scenics' foam incline and riser components.

Figure-eight schemes can be more than just a gimmick. Here, a 5½-inch-high overpass helps keep trains in continuous motion, without the peril of operating through a 90-degree crossing.

A passing siding doesn't have to be on the straight and narrow. In this instance, I placed a train-length siding along a curve. It's near the outer edge of the layout, so restricted speed operation is a must. Don't forget, you can also use this location to reverse the direction of your train—just be sure to use a locomotive with operating couplers on each end.

repeated, but another option is provided by a passing siding bent around the second curve. Park a train heading uphill along the siding, and you've got the main line cleared for a second train or maintenance-of-way work.

To establish the mountainous terrain for this layout, I'd suggest stacking a single sheet of 2-inch-thick foam insulation board over lightweight benchwork or even a sheet of plywood. Assemble the plan on the top surface and trace the position of

each FasTrack section. Then, after you remove the connected track, you can use a hot knife or fine-tooth pull saw to carve additional pieces of foam board needed to build up the elevation both under and alongside the track. Even simpler, just use precut foam riser and incline (4 percent) sets from Woodland Scenics—and get to the thrill of running toy trains over a mountain pass on a 4 x 8-foot layout much quicker!

By Kent Johnson

LIONEL FASTRACK COMPONENTS

Quantity	Description/Number
2	1.75-inch straight (12026)
1	4.5-inch straight (12025)
6	10-inch straight (12014)
14	0-36 curve, 45-degree (12015)
3	0-36 curve, 22.5-degree (12022)
3	0-36 curve, 11.25-degree (12023)
3	0-36 left-hand track switch (12045)
1	0-36 right-hand track switch (12046)
1	bumper (12059)

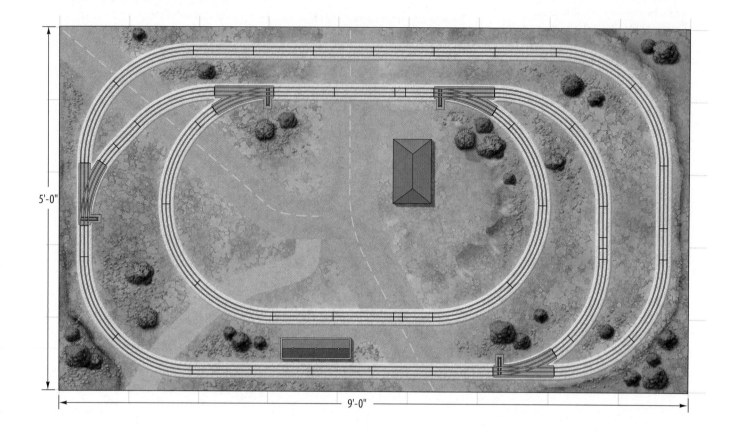

5'-0"

9'-0"

Biggerboard Railroad Co.

From its earliest origins to present day, the most common dimension for a typical O gauge starter layout remains 4 x 8 feet. It's more than a happy accident that this dimension is identical to a single sheet of ¾-inch plywood, which also happens to be the most common material used to construct a new layout.

But while a single sheet of plywood fits neatly into the back of Pop's pickup truck or Ma's mini van, this easy-to-haul

material can be restrictive for developing a full-featured O gauge layout. The need for a little more space than a 4 x 8 sheet had to offer became apparent with the introduction of the Lionel FasTrack system, featuring 36-inch diameter curves that are slightly larger than traditional 31-inch diameter curves.

This plan offers one solution to the dilemma by simply adding another foot of real estate along two sides of the scheme. The resulting adaptation affords FasTrack

users enough space to host desirable twin, or even triple, loops of track needed to operate two trains at the same time!

Although there isn't a single 5 x 9 sheet of plywood to suit this type of expansion, options for easily constructing the required layout framework can be found in various publications, including *Basic Model Railroad Benchwork, Second Edition* (Kalmbach Books, 2012).

By Kent Johnson

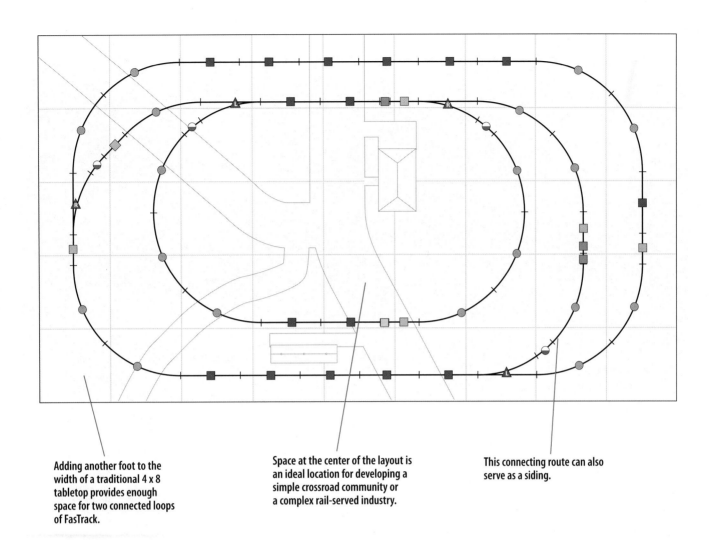

Adding another foot to the width of a traditional 4 x 8 tabletop provides enough space for two connected loops of FasTrack.

Space at the center of the layout is an ideal location for developing a simple crossroad community or a complex rail-served industry.

This connecting route can also serve as a siding.

LIONEL FASTRACK COMPONENTS

Quantity	Description/Number
1	1.375-inch straight (12073)
3	1.75-inch straight (12026)
6	5-inch straight (12024)
16	10-inch straight (12014)
4	O-36 curve, 11.25-degree (12023)
18	O-36 curve, 45-degree (12015)
2	O-36 left-hand track switch (12045)
2	O-36 right-hand track switch (12046)

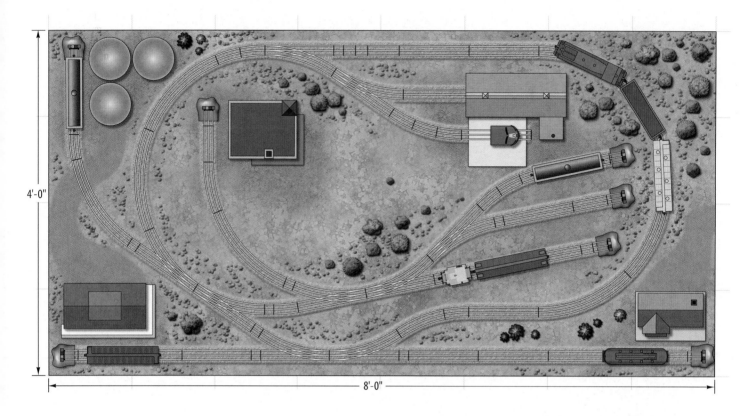

Industrial Mite

An Allegheny, a Big Boy, a Centipede, and a DD40X. They make up just a sampling of the gargantuan O gauge locomotive offerings that have inspired toy train operators to plan and sometimes build layouts of equally epic proportions. But how many of us are motivated to think small when we're enamored of a diminutive diesel or slight steamer?

Although I initially had doubts about this approach, the process of building CTT's Readers' Choice Railroad (see pages 5–9) helped convince me otherwise. After operating Ready Made Trains by Aristo-Craft (RMT) Beep locomotives on the 4 x 8-foot O gauge layout, I began to see how a compact layout might complement a tiny train. Then, with the arrival of the Lionel 28450 CP Rail Trackmobile, I was ready and rarin' to start planning a small, yet fully functional, O gauge layout specifically intended for this Industrial Mite.

Down to size

I started sketching this track plan with the thought that a basic point-to-point scheme might be the most appropriate environment for my new favorite motorized unit. But even though I enjoyed operating the Trackmobile in the Readers' Choice layout extension (see pages 57–59), I wondered if most operators would soon long for a continuous route. That's when I challenged myself to design a small layout featuring both types of operation.

Working within the borders of a single 4 x 8-foot sheet of plywood, I included several rail-served industries, a locomotive and car maintenance facility, a yard, and a loop of track that permits unimpeded operation. A loop of broader O-36 curves and track switches extends to the outer edges of the tabletop, but the ability to run more standard-sized trains made the decision easier to endure.

Moving freight cars

The Trackmobile is best suited for shunting one or two cars from the compact, three-track yard to any of the three distinct industries. By design, it can access

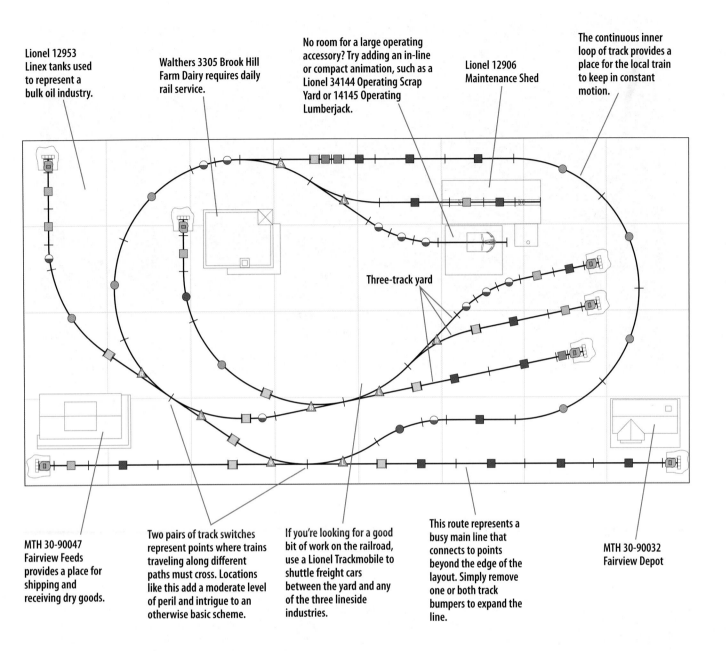

Lionel 12953 Linex tanks used to represent a bulk oil industry.

Walthers 3305 Brook Hill Farm Dairy requires daily rail service.

No room for a large operating accessory? Try adding an in-line or compact animation, such as a Lionel 34144 Operating Scrap Yard or 14145 Operating Lumberjack.

Lionel 12906 Maintenance Shed

The continuous inner loop of track provides a place for the local train to keep in constant motion.

Three-track yard

MTH 30-90047 Fairview Feeds provides a place for shipping and receiving dry goods.

Two pairs of track switches represent points where trains traveling along different paths must cross. Locations like this add a moderate level of peril and intrigue to an otherwise basic scheme.

If you're looking for a good bit of work on the railroad, use a Lionel Trackmobile to shuttle freight cars between the yard and any of the three lineside industries.

This route represents a busy main line that connects to points beyond the edge of the layout. Simply remove one or both track bumpers to expand the line.

MTH 30-90032 Fairview Depot

two of the three industrial sidings without traversing the mainline loop. An operator can make a job out of swapping empty cars with loaded ones and then return the unit to the maintenance facility at the end of the day.

Next, it's time for the local job, perhaps led by a small diesel switcher, to drop off and pick up freight cars spotted in the yard. That's where the continuous operation over the loop of track comes into play.

Of course, the ultimate challenge is to perform both jobs at the same time, which is possible if you've wired the layout for control using two separate electrical blocks

and a transformer with twin throttles or if you've installed a command control system.

Despite the industrial slant to this O gauge layout, there's plenty of opportunity to incorporate passenger service. Perhaps the simplest option is to add a trolley equipped with a bumper reverse mechanism. Set it on the main line at the front edge of the layout, and you've effectively added a third train to the action. If you prefer a more versatile mainline people mover, a Budd Rail Diesel Car is ideal for getting laborers closer to the industries along this not-so-big yet bustling scheme.

By Kent Johnson

LIONEL FASTRACK COMPONENTS

Quantity	Description/Number
9	1.375-inch fitter (12000X)
3	1.75-inch straight (12026)
3	4.5-inch straight (12025)
7	5-inch straight (12024)
12	10-inch straight (12014)
8	0-36 curve, 45-degree (12015)
2	0-36 curve, 22.5-degree (12022)
11	0-36 curve, 11.25-degree (12023)
4	0-36 left-hand manual switch (12017)
5	0-36 right-hand manual switch (12018)
8	bumper (12059)

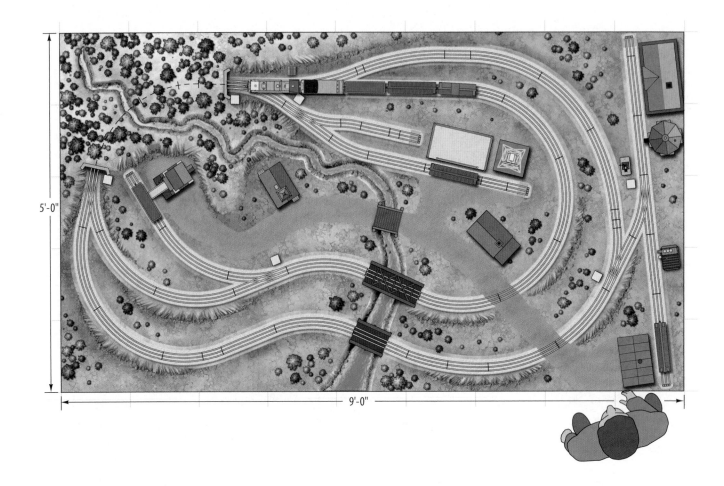

5'-0"

9'-0"

Copper Valley Ry.

The vast expanse of America's western regions probably isn't the first thing you'd expect to re-create in a space that's only slightly larger than a sheet of plywood. But before you dismiss the possibility of an O gauge layout that's born of the Old West, you'll want to explore the features of this 5- by 9-foot track plan.

Based on an HO scale scheme for the Hazzard County Short Line (*48 Top Notch*

Track Plans, Kalmbach Books, 1993) and inspired by recent O gauge models of 19th century American railroad equipment, this plan features rugged western scenery and plenty of rootin', tootin' railroad action to boot. The hills contain a copper mine, a bubbling mountain brook, and high-country landscape dotted with Ponderosa pines. The railroad battles the terrain, the elements, and sometimes even robbers!

Although this plan features a continuous oval design, it's not likely you'll forget the railroad exists to keep supplies, people, and livestock headed into the western frontier. Take a close look at the shifting high line route—assembled from O-36, O-48, and O-72 FasTrack curve sections and laid on a variable 2 to 4 percent grade—and you'll begin to appreciate exactly how wild a train ride into the Old West must have been.

Old West trains
On a route this treacherous, you'll want to be sure you're operating the appropriate equipment. Lionel's postwar *General* 4-4-0 steam locomotives and mixed train sets may have been the first to fit the period and locale, but today, others are also available.

One Lionel set you might consider using is the 30116 Lone Ranger set. The

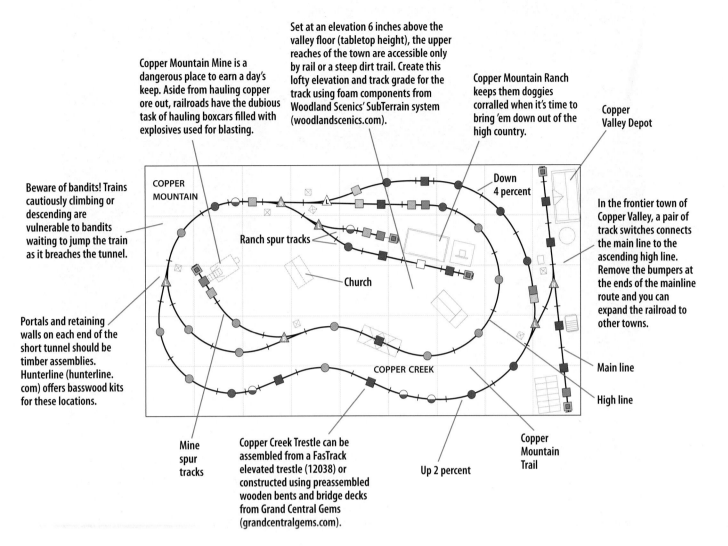

Copper Mountain Mine is a dangerous place to earn a day's keep. Aside from hauling copper ore out, railroads have the dubious task of hauling boxcars filled with explosives used for blasting.

Set at an elevation 6 inches above the valley floor (tabletop height), the upper reaches of the town are accessible only by rail or a steep dirt trail. Create this lofty elevation and track grade for the track using foam components from Woodland Scenics' SubTerrain system (woodlandscenics.com).

Copper Mountain Ranch keeps them doggies corralled when it's time to bring 'em down out of the high country.

Copper Valley Depot

Beware of bandits! Trains cautiously climbing or descending are vulnerable to bandits waiting to jump the train as it breaches the tunnel.

COPPER MOUNTAIN

Ranch spur tracks

Church

Down 4 percent

In the frontier town of Copper Valley, a pair of track switches connects the main line to the ascending high line. Remove the bumpers at the ends of the mainline route and you can expand the railroad to other towns.

Portals and retaining walls on each end of the short tunnel should be timber assemblies. Hunterline (hunterline. com) offers basswood kits for these locations.

COPPER CREEK

Main line

High line

Mine spur tracks

Copper Creek Trestle can be assembled from a FasTrack elevated trestle (12038) or constructed using preassembled wooden bents and bridge decks from Grand Central Gems (grandcentralgems.com).

Up 2 percent

Copper Mountain Trail

Lone Ranger rides again aboard a train that includes a period 4-4-0 locomotive, passenger coach, gondola, and operating Lone Ranger and outlaw car. The set also includes FasTrack sections, figures, and a transformer.

MTH's RailKing and Premier lines offer a broad range of items that would've worked the western rails in the mid to late 19th century, including 4-4-0, 4-6-0, and 2-8-0 steam locomotives, assorted freight car types, and Overton passenger cars.

If it's museum-quality detail you're after, SMR Trains (smrtrains.com) offers historically accurate, scale versions of the 4-4-0 American-type locomotive.

The only other requirement for constructing this Old Wild West layout is your imagination—westward ho!

By Kent Johnson

SUGGESTED ACCESSORIES

Lionel

Number	Product
2175	Gravel loader
12718	Barrel shed
12734	Passenger/freight station
12773	Freight platform
12828	Stockyard
12889	Motorized windmill
22944	Semaphore
62716	Short extension bridge

MTH

Number	Product
30-9002	Country church
30-11028	Water tower
30-90008	Work house

LIONEL FASTRACK COMPONENTS

Quantity		Description/Number
3		1.38-inch fitter
5		1.75-inch straight (12026)
2		4.5-inch straight (12025)
4		5-inch straight (12024)
9		10-inch straight (12014)
3		O-36 curve, 11.25-degree (12023)
4		O-36 curve, 22.5-degree (12022)
4		O-48 curve, 30-degree (12043)
2		O-72 curve, 22.5-degree (12041)
2		O-72 curve, 11.25-degree (12055)
12		O-36 curve, 45-degree (12015)
3		O-36 left-hand track switch, manual (12017)
3		O-36 right-hand track switch, manual (12018)
1		O-60 left-hand track switch (12057)
1		operating track (12054)
5		track bumper (12059)

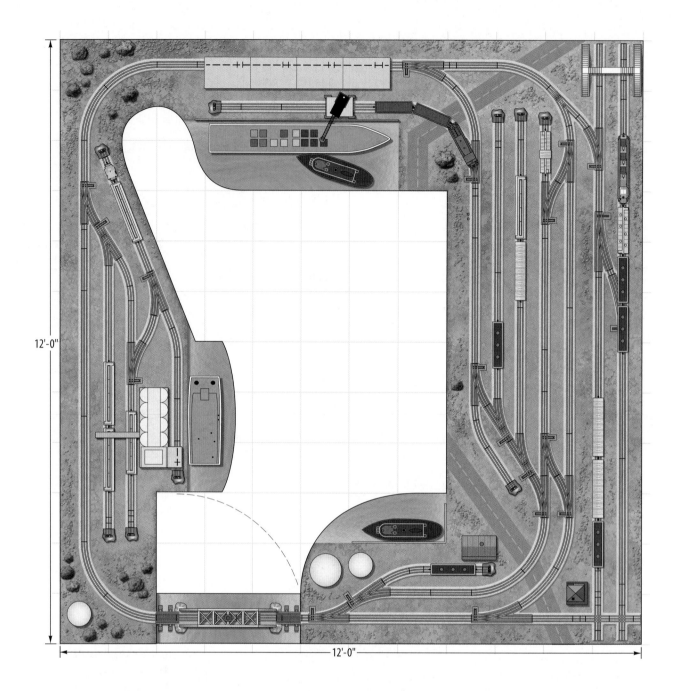

12'-0"

12'-0"

Docks Ry.

Water, water, everywhere, plus plenty of railroading action to follow along its shores! That's the premise of this 12 x 12-foot track plan. The plan leaves the middle of the scheme vacant to represent open water, and it positions a continuous network of FasTrack rails tight against four walls.

The introduction of a few Lionel products has made it much easier to capture

the character of a waterfront railroad on an O gauge layout. Perhaps the most significant contribution to the marine theme is the broad line of Lionel tugboats. While measuring less than 20 inches long, the presence of one or more of these tugs implies that there are even larger vessels arriving and departing nearby ports of call, even if they aren't modeled!

But when it comes to modeling the rails along the shore, using FasTrack

makes it possible to closely align the tracks needed to form compact yards and to route the tight curves of the waterfront branch around portside industries and warehouses.

Although the track plan has a high concentration of tight trackwork, that doesn't mean it's strictly a back-and-forth switching affair. In addition to the continuous, around-the-walls waterfront branch route, the plan includes an interchange with the

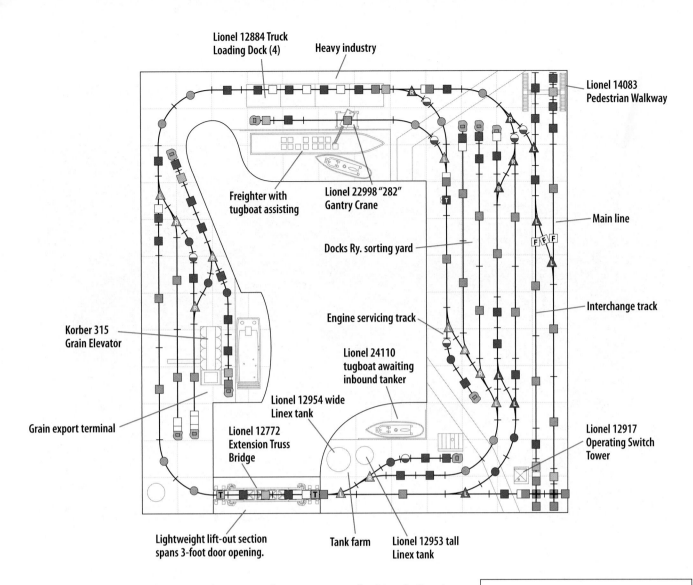

Lionel 12884 Truck Loading Dock (4)

Heavy industry

Lionel 14083 Pedestrian Walkway

Freighter with tugboat assisting

Lionel 22998 "282" Gantry Crane

Main line

Docks Ry. sorting yard

Interchange track

Korber 315 Grain Elevator

Engine servicing track

Lionel 24110 tugboat awaiting inbound tanker

Grain export terminal

Lionel 12954 wide Linex tank

Lionel 12772 Extension Truss Bridge

Lionel 12917 Operating Switch Tower

Lightweight lift-out section spans 3-foot door opening.

Tank farm

Lionel 12953 tall Linex tank

mainline tracks of a larger, farther-reaching railroad.

Running trains

You'll need to first walk through the room door and place a 1 x 3-foot removable section across the opening to form a continuous, water-level (no grade) loop. I designed this section with FasTrack transition pieces fitted on the ends, so it is easier to lift out. Power for the lift-out track section routes through a modified trailer wiring harness with quick-connect ends.

With the section in place, the operation begins when a road switcher delivers freight cars from the main line to the interchange track. A smaller Docks Ry. switcher departs for the small yard to retrieve these cars from the interchange and begin the sorting process. Once cars are in order, the switcher heads out over the waterfront branch line. The first stop is a tank farm, where you can position tank cars. A large coastal tanker isn't needed to

set the scene—just a few Lionel oil tanks and some waiting tank cars.

As the train departs yard limits, it rolls over the lift-out section and heads to the grain elevator. The Docks Ry. switcher needs only to exchange loaded grain hoppers for empty cars. A tiny Lionel Trackmobile handles all other duties at this terminal, which creates an ideal position for a second operator with a handheld Lionel CAB-2 that controls a Lionel Legacy command control system.

Continuous fun

The train makes it way to the final stop, a heavy industry with portside loading via a gantry crane. The switcher drops off open-load freight cars (flat cars or gondolas) alongside an outbound freighter, and then it heads for home with empty cars. Even though the train has reached the end of the line, it also represents the starting point for a continuous cycle of toy train operating fun!

By Kent Johnson

LIONEL FASTRACK COMPONENTS

Quantity		Description/Number
3	F	1.375-inch fitter straight (12000X)
16		1.375-inch straight (12073)
10		1.75-inch straight (12026)
8		4.5-inch straight (12025)
8		5-inch straight (12024)
31		10-inch straight (12014)
20		30-inch straight (12042)
7		0-36 curve, 11.25-degree (12023)
5		0-36 curve, 22.5-degree (12022)
9		0-36 curve, 45-degree (12015)
2		0-48 curve, 30-degree (12043)
5		0-36 left-hand manual switch (12017)
6		0-36 right-hand manual switch (12018)
3		0-36 left-hand remote switch (12045)
4	R	0-36 right-hand remote switch (12046)
1		0-48 left-hand remote switch (12065)
2		0-72 left-hand remote switch (12048)
1	T	10-inch terminal straight (12016)
2	T	10-inch transition straight (12040)
2		crossing, 90-degree (12019)
10		bumper (12059)

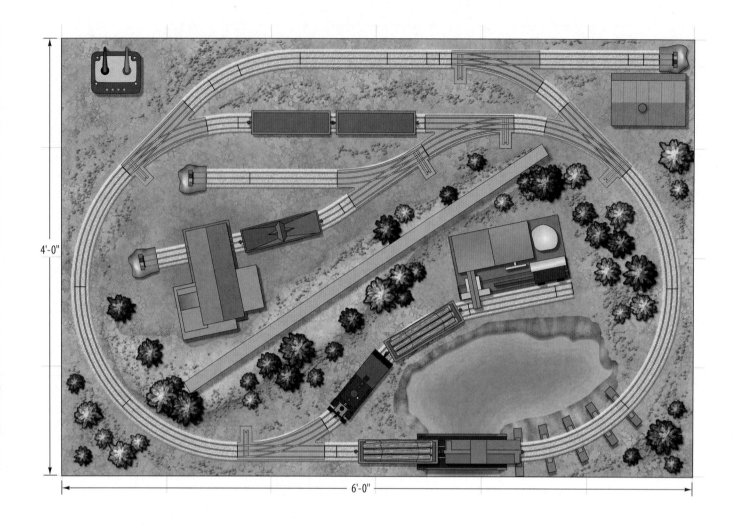

4'-0"

6'-0"

Gold Hill Central

After recently constructing a 4 x 8-foot project layout for *Classic Toy Trains* magazine, I realized that even a small O gauge arrangement could quickly fill up a significant portion of a typical household bedroom. I found that while a small layout might only occupy a finite area of a room, you must still leave room to access all points of the pike. In the case of our project layout, that meant leaving at least a 2-foot perimeter around each side. It didn't take long to calculate that this additional "working room" immediately expands the layout area from 4 x 8-feet to 8 x 12-feet.

I can only imagine the trouble I'd encounter trying to explain to my spouse how a small 32 square-foot layout now requires a 96 square-foot space! While there are many effective techniques for begging and pleading for more space, there's only one way to make things work and leave your dignity intact—shrink a 4 x 8-foot layout down to size. And that's precisely what I did to this compact Fas-Track plan for the Gold Hill Central.

Simply by trimming the excess tabletop area from an otherwise full-featured 4 x 8-foot design, I was able to fit standard FasTrack O-36 curves into a 4 x 6-foot

space. Now when you add on the 2-foot working-room perimeter, the overall area holds steady at 80 square feet. So what did I have to sacrifice to make it all work, you ask? Nothing (other than a wee bit of my dignity)!

Pint-sized pike packs a punch

Everything you'd expect to find on a small layout can be found on the 4 x 6-foot Gold Hill Central, a railroad serving gold mining and logging industries in the western United States. Since the action isn't fast paced in and around the two industrial areas, separated by a 2-foot-tall view block

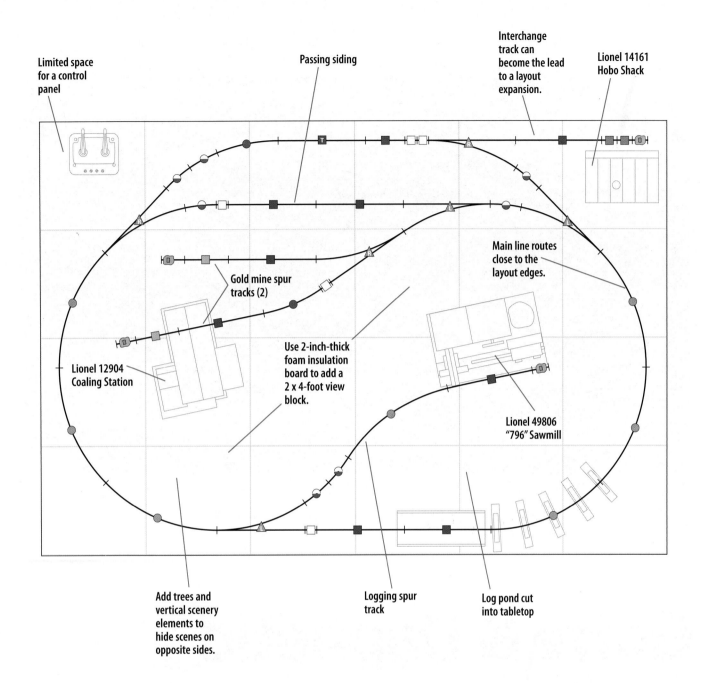

Limited space for a control panel

Passing siding

Interchange track can become the lead to a layout expansion.

Lionel 14161 Hobo Shack

Gold mine spur tracks (2)

Main line routes close to the layout edges.

Use 2-inch-thick foam insulation board to add a 2 x 4-foot view block.

Lionel 12904 Coaling Station

Lionel 49806 "796" Sawmill

Add trees and vertical scenery elements to hide scenes on opposite sides.

Logging spur track

Log pond cut into tabletop

set diagonally on the slimmed down tabletop, I didn't worry much about setting the O-36 curves right along the layout edges. Using the recently released FasTrack O-31 curves is another way to pull the main line back from the edges. However, other extreme modifications would also be necessary to pair the O-31 curves with standard O-36 track switches.

Looking even closer at the layout elements, you'll find that the Gold Hill plan includes spur tracks for both industries. There are actually two spurs at the gold—one for loading ore cars and the other for storing and servicing a small

steam-powered switcher (0-4-0, 0-6-0). In addition to the industrial spurs, there's also a passing siding that allows a second train to route around the switcher working the gold mine.

Too much to be true? Not yet! Along the main line, this plan also features an interchange track. By itself, this short section of track is only long enough to hold a few small ore or log cars. But if you do manage to obtain additional space beyond 80 square feet, this section of track becomes the physical link to an expanded railroad.

By Kent Johnson

LIONEL FASTRACK COMPONENTS

Quantity	Description/Number
5	☐ 1.375-inch straight (12073)
2	▣ 1.75-inch straight (12026)
1	■ 4.5-inch straight (12025)
2	▣ 5-inch straight (12024)
8	■ 10-inch straight (12014)
1	Ⓣ 10-inch terminal straight (12016)
7	◖ 0-36 curve, 11.25-degree (12023)
2	● 0-36 curve, 22.5-degree (12022)
7	● 0-36 curve, 45-degree (12015)
3	△ 0-36 left-hand manual switch (12017)
3	⚠ 0-36 right-hand manual switch (12018)
4	▣ bumper (12059)

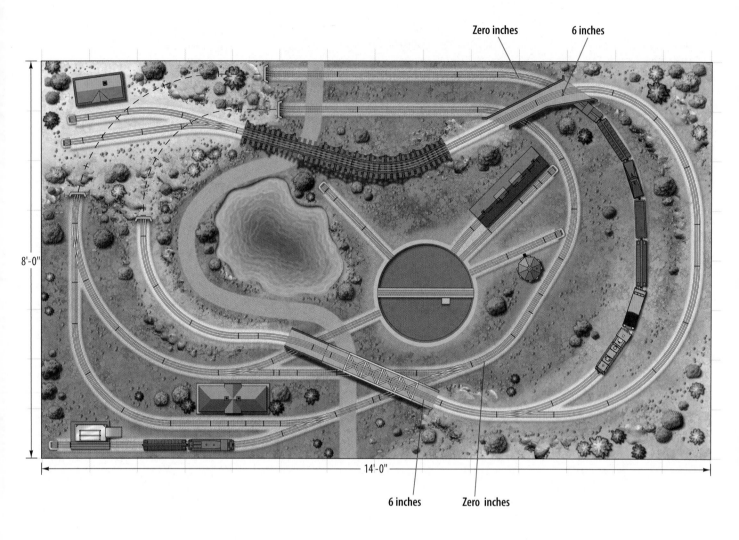

Zero inches   6 inches

8'-0"

6 inches   Zero inches

14'-0"

Gorre & Daphetid

The track plan shown here is famed model railroader John Allen's first HO scale Gorre & Daphetid layout, which dates to the late 1940s. John, as many hobbyists know, was a groundbreaking model railroader who inspired literally tens of thousands of layout builders with his serious, yet whimsical Gorre & Daphetid Railroad (pronounced *gory and defeated*).

While many hobbyists recall his rugged floor-to-ceiling scenery and soaring bridges thanks to dozens of photos published in model railroading magazines over three decades, not all realize that the origin of his 24- by 32-foot empire was an

up-and-over oval smaller than a sheet of plywood. John built it before he moved to a hillside California residence that became home to the ultimate Gorre & Daphetid layout.

This track plan fits into an 8- by 14-foot space and is fairly faithful to the original (featured in *101 Track Plans for Model Railroaders*, Kalmbach Books, 1956). However, some small tweaks were necessary to adopt John's plan to sectional track.

Enlarging the original HO plan to O gauge has put the center of the layout well beyond arm's length. At the very least, you'll want to make the lake bed a hinged

access hatch or omit the water material as a matter of convenience.

Adapting FasTrack
FasTrack is tricky to work with for this plan. FasTrack curves, like other types of sectional track, follow a specific geometry in which standard curve sections are measured in increments of 22.5, 30, or 45 degrees.

For example, four 45-degree curves would equal a half circle (180 degrees) and six 30-degree curves would equal a half circle. But a rambling half circle made of three 45-degree curves and two 30-degree curves will never equal a complete

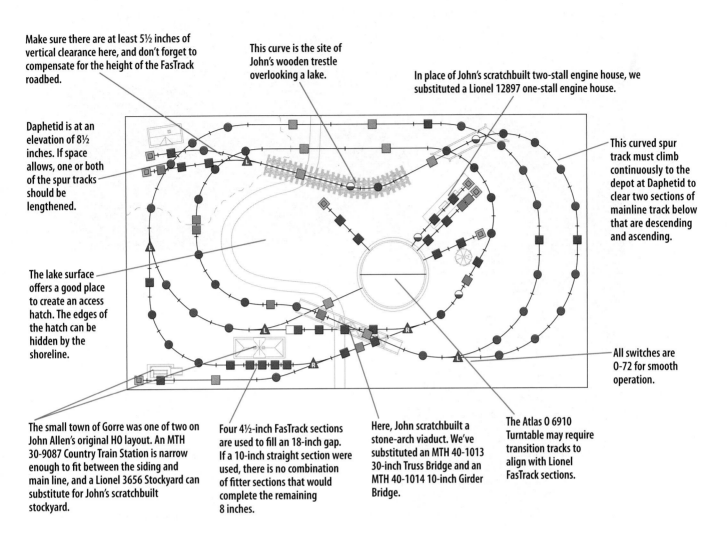

Make sure there are at least 5½ inches of vertical clearance here, and don't forget to compensate for the height of the FasTrack roadbed.

This curve is the site of John's wooden trestle overlooking a lake.

In place of John's scratchbuilt two-stall engine house, we substituted a Lionel 12897 one-stall engine house.

Daphetid is at an elevation of 8½ inches. If space allows, one or both of the spur tracks should be lengthened.

This curved spur track must climb continuously to the depot at Daphetid to clear two sections of mainline track below that are descending and ascending.

The lake surface offers a good place to create an access hatch. The edges of the hatch can be hidden by the shoreline.

All switches are 0-72 for smooth operation.

The small town of Gorre was one of two on John Allen's original HO layout. An MTH 30-9087 Country Train Station is narrow enough to fit between the siding and main line, and a Lionel 3656 Stockyard can substitute for John's scratchbuilt stockyard.

Four 4½-inch FasTrack sections are used to fill an 18-inch gap. If a 10-inch straight section were used, there is no combination of fitter sections that would complete the remaining 8 inches.

Here, John scratchbuilt a stone-arch viaduct. We've substituted an MTH 40-1013 30-inch Truss Bridge and an MTH 40-1014 10-inch Girder Bridge.

The Atlas O 6910 Turntable may require transition tracks to align with Lionel FasTrack sections.

180-degree turn without having to turn to a hacksaw.

Keeping faithful to the original Gorre & Daphetid requires an asymmetrical mix of FasTrack O-48 (30-degree) curves and O-72 (22.5-degree) curves. Mixing those sections means everything doesn't always add up to 180 or 360 degrees, resulting in some joints where the track needs to be fudged just a tiny bit to connect. On this plan, there are enough track joints surrounding the fudged areas (in front of the Gorre depot and just to the right of the turntable) to get the job done.

By Neil Besougloff

SUGGESTED ACCESSORIES

Atlas O

Number	Product
6910	Turntable

Lionel

Number	Product
12734	Passenger/freight station
12773	Freight platform
12897	Engine house
14086	"38" water tower

MTH

Number	Product
30-9087	Country train station
40-1013	30-inch truss bridge
40-1014	10-inch girder bridge

LIONEL FASTRACK COMPONENTS

Quantity	Description/Number
1	1.38-inch fitter
3	1.75-inch straight (12026)
5	4.5-inch straight (12025)
6	5-inch straight (12024)
23	10-inch straight (12014)
9	30-inch straight (12042)
17	0-48 curve, 30-degree (12043)
4	0-72 curve, 11.25-degree (12055)
24	0-72 curve, 22.5-degree (12041)
4	0-72 left-hand track switch (12048)
2	0-72 right-hand track switch (12049)
7	track bumper (12059)

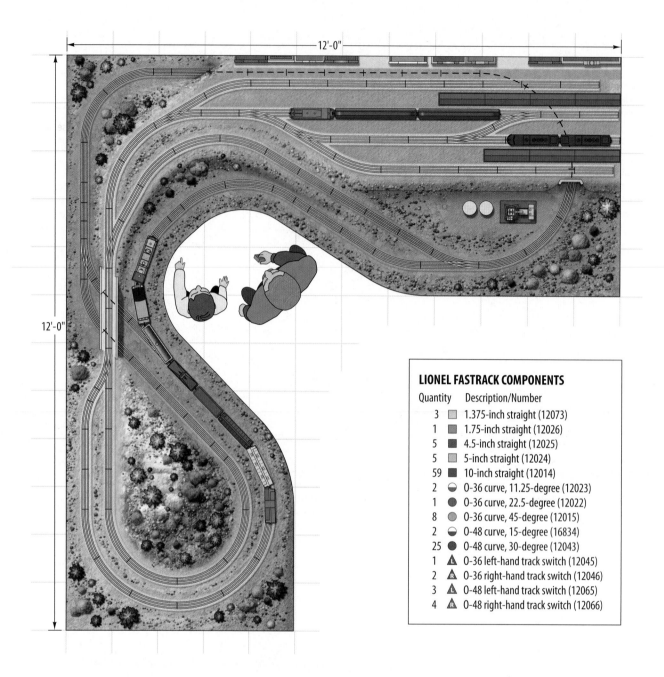

12'-0"

12'-0"

LIONEL FASTRACK COMPONENTS

Quantity		Description/Number
3		1.375-inch straight (12073)
1		1.75-inch straight (12026)
5		4.5-inch straight (12025)
5		5-inch straight (12024)
59		10-inch straight (12014)
2		O-36 curve, 11.25-degree (12023)
1		O-36 curve, 22.5-degree (12022)
8		O-36 curve, 45-degree (12015)
2		O-48 curve, 15-degree (16834)
25		O-48 curve, 30-degree (12043)
1		O-36 left-hand track switch (12045)
2		O-36 right-hand track switch (12046)
3		O-48 left-hand track switch (12065)
4		O-48 right-hand track switch (12066)

Modified Figure Eight

Looking for a room-sized layout with space for scenery, room for trains to roll, plus a passenger depot or freight yard? Then this 12 x 12-foot track plan may be exactly right for you.

While the plan forms an L shape, it's actually a modified figure-eight scheme, with an overpass at the center of the action. The cutoff that runs along the front of the layout lets you run out and back,

and a passing siding allows for running one train in both directions or two trains in the same direction. About the only thing this design doesn't have is an area that's filled with accessories, although it would be simple to add a few in the rail yard.

Any track that's on a grade is at the front of the layout, and all the track switches (O-36 and O-48) are within arm's

reach. There's one hidden track under the town area, but you can easily construct the benchwork to provide access to that track from underneath. The town area can be built as a four-track passenger station, a four-track yard, or some combination of the two. Use the two tracks with the locomotive escape crossover for arrivals and the other two tracks for departures or as your coach yard.

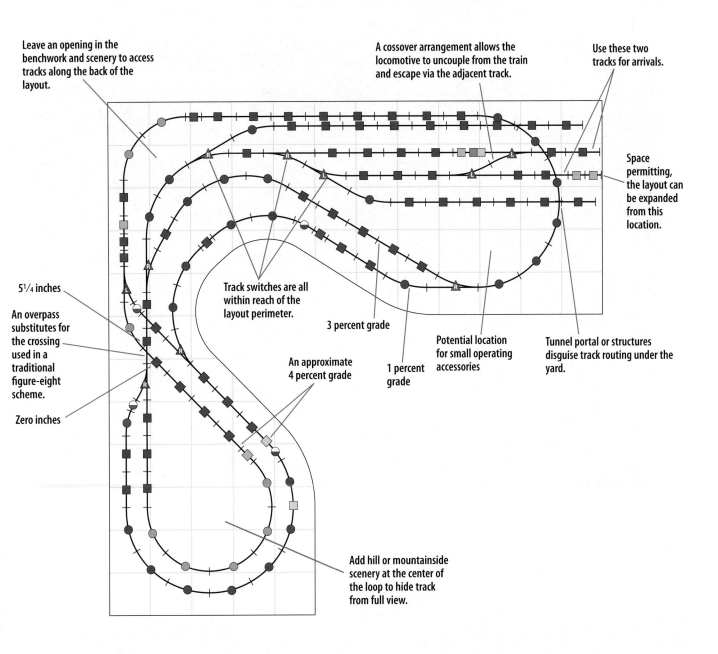

Leave an opening in the benchwork and scenery to access tracks along the back of the layout.

A cossover arrangement allows the locomotive to uncouple from the train and escape via the adjacent track.

Use these two tracks for arrivals.

Space permitting, the layout can be expanded from this location.

5¼ inches

An overpass substitutes for the crossing used in a traditional figure-eight scheme.

Zero inches

Track switches are all within reach of the layout perimeter.

3 percent grade

An approximate 4 percent grade

1 percent grade

Potential location for small operating accessories

Tunnel portal or structures disguise track routing under the yard.

Add hill or mountainside scenery at the center of the loop to hide track from full view.

The only way to turn a locomotive is by using the cutoff track and one of the loops. However, it is a simple project to extend the benchwork a bit on the right and add a turntable, perhaps with a roundhouse.

To get this much operation into the space, I needed to include a few O-36 curves and design the grade on the inner track of the left-hand loop to nearly 4 percent. The other grades are more forgiving.

The wiring can be simply one transformer with on/off switches for the yard tracks, passing siding, and cutoff tracks. This way you can run two trains, although not at the same time.

Building the layout

If I were building this layout, I would probably choose an eastern theme and use a hill in the center of the left-hand loop to

add some interest to the scenery. Of course, western scenery would work just as well.

Either way, you'll have a fun, scenic layout that fits in a space of roughly 100 square feet, leaving nearly 50 square feet of room for a desk and chair—or, better still, an easy chair and a TV, so you can watch those trains go by as you catch the game.

By Terry Thompson

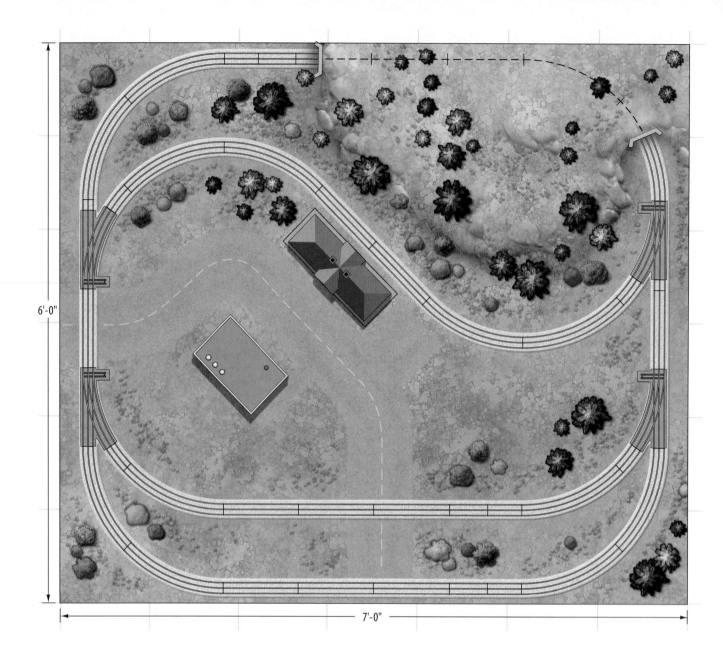

6'-0"

7'-0"

Reversible Roundabout

Who says a circle of track can't provide countless hours of enjoyment? Even though this 6 x 7-foot plan appears more akin to a rectangle than a circle, it's hard to characterize this roundabout design as square. Just take a closer look at the components of this scheme, and you'll see two features that make this plan so much more sophisticated than a circling arrangement.

The first element that elevates this plan beyond basic is the inclusion of a reverse loop. With the addition of two right-hand track switches, four curves, and two straight sections, an operator can easily change a train's clockwise direction to counterclockwise—all without uncoupling the locomotive or removing cars from the track.

Additionally, a second pair of track switches (left-hand) and a handful of

straight sections help create a place to park a second train without keeping another from making the rounds.

Looking beyond the initial arrangement, you'll see that there's still plenty of space remaining to add a small yard or industrial spur at the center of the layout. If scenery is more desirable, then you might consider adding a hillside or mountain at the center to partially conceal the reverse loop.

By Kent Johnson

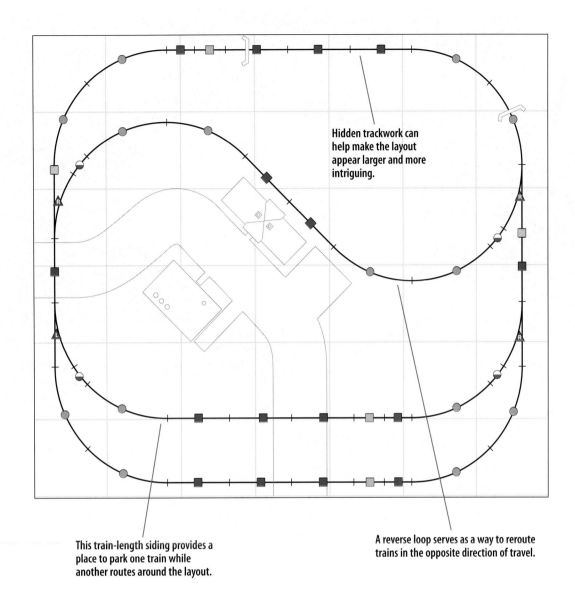

Hidden trackwork can help make the layout appear larger and more intriguing.

This train-length siding provides a place to park one train while another routes around the layout.

A reverse loop serves as a way to reroute trains in the opposite direction of travel.

LIONEL FASTRACK COMPONENTS

Quantity	Description/Number
2	1.375-inch straight (12073)
3	4.5-inch straight (12025)
3	5-inch straight (12024)
13	10-inch straight (12014)
4	O-36 curve, 11.25-degree (12023)
14	O-36 curve, 45-degree (12015)
1	O-36 left-hand track switch (12045)
3	O-36 right-hand track switch (12046)

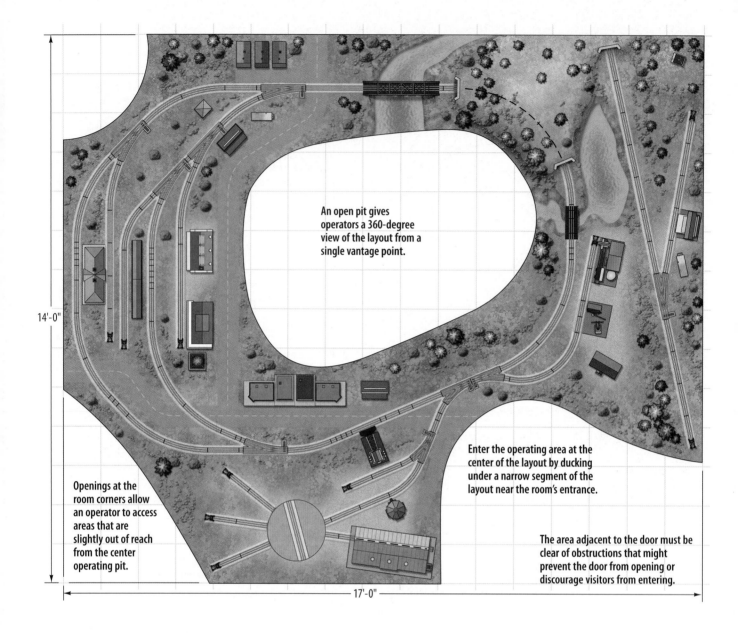

An open pit gives operators a 360-degree view of the layout from a single vantage point.

14'-0"

Openings at the room corners allow an operator to access areas that are slightly out of reach from the center operating pit.

Enter the operating area at the center of the layout by ducking under a narrow segment of the layout near the room's entrance.

The area adjacent to the door must be clear of obstructions that might prevent the door from opening or discourage visitors from entering.

17'-0"

Logging Lines Central

Incorporating log dump cars, log loaders, and a sawmill, this track plan provides the foundation for a layout that features big-time logging operations. It also keeps you right in the middle of the railroad action.

This layout is derived from a track plan, the Lumber City Limited, originally published in Lionel's *Model Builder* magazine during the 1940s.

Although the track plan has been redesigned using Lionel FasTrack instead of tubular track, the 14 x 17-foot dimensions

of this plan match those of the original Lumber City Limited layout.

Rather than maintaining the original tabletop design, the Logging Lines Central features a duckunder that provides access to an operating area in the middle of the layout. With an around-the-walls scheme, operators using a wireless command control system can easily follow and access trains moving around the perimeter.

One benefit to having the main operating area in the center of the layout is having additional space available for

more track and scenery. Once only a simple loop of track, the logging branch can now become a steep, mountainous switchback route that's ideal for showcasing a Shay, Heisler, Climax, or other geared steam locomotive. Although the logging operation will keep you plenty busy, there's still another complete railroad to run.

Mainline action

The mainline action starts right as you walk through the door. There, you'll find a locomotive servicing terminal designed to use a 20" turntable, a large back shop, coal elevator, water tower, and three stalls to hold semi-scale steam locomotives and their tenders. If contemporary railroading is more to your liking, you can easily swap the steam power for moderately sized diesels.

With the motive power ready for action, the work of the railroad awaits. Located on a spur just a few FasTrack O-36 switches away from the servicing facility, the operating sawmill and forklift platform provide plenty of lumber loads to haul. Couple your engine to the flatcars or boxcars spotted on the mill spur, and you're set to move 'em out.

But before you leave the mill, you may want to venture up into the high country. There, a geared steam locomotive, or even an SW8 diesel switcher, brings tall timber down from an upper mountain logging camp. When the train of log dump cars reaches the bottom of the switchback route, it dumps the logs into the mill pond and heads back up to repeat the process.

In the middle

If you think the view from the base of the mill operation is interesting, just duck under the layout and move into the center of the room. From this location, you'll be able to follow a train through forested mountain scenery, into tunnels, and over waterways on its way around the gently sweeping FasTrack O-72 curves.

The busy mill town on the far side of the layout isn't large, yet it still maintains a serviceable warehouse, company feed and supply store, and a few sidings ideal for dropping off freight cars bound for industries farther down the line.

Upon arrival, loggers and their families will appreciate the quaint but respectable depot and platforms. For those who have escaped the row house accommodations at the outskirts of town, a daily doodlebug or Budd Rail Diesel Car special arrives and departs from the station's two passenger train sidings. Trains rolling out of town will pass only a handful of stores on Main Street, but each business, like the railroad, serves the town well.

Even though the best vantage point is from the center of the room, there's still space in three corners to access your trains, add a workbench, or just enjoy a new perspective of the Logging Lines Central on the go.

By E.A. Engebretson and Kent Johnson

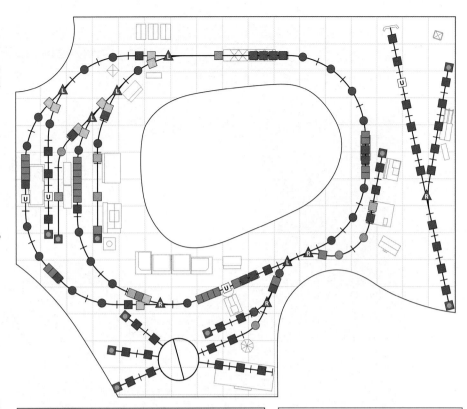

SUGGESTED ACCESSORIES

Lionel

Number	Product
96/97	Coal elevator
12772	Extension truss bridge
12774	Lumber loader
12878	Illuminated control tower
12916	Water tower
14000	"264" forklift platform
14154	"193" water tower
22907	Die-cast girder bridge
22918	Locomotive repair
49806	"23796" sawmill

MTH

Number	Product
30-9006	Passenger station platform
30-9023	Row house
30-9024	Row house
30-9051	Myersville station
30-9076	Row house
30-9088	Vegetable stand
30-9093	Fireworks stand
30-9098	Warehouse
30-9107	Operating station platform
30-90005	Mobile home (2)
30-90006	Yard tower
30-90019	Lombardi's Pizza
30-90020	Katz's Deli
30-90022	Jenny Lee Bakery
30-90023	Soda Fountain
30-90024	Thomas & Sons Feeds
30-90037	Elk River Logging Co.

Bowser	20-inch turntable

LIONEL FASTRACK COMPONENTS

Quantity	Description/Number
10	1.38-inch straight (with 12048/49)
26	1.75-inch straight (12026)
11	4.5-inch straight (12025)
3	5-inch straight (12024)
3	5-inch uncoupling track (12020)
37	10-inch straight (12014)
4	10-inch uncoupling track (12054)
3	30-inch straight (12042)
4	O-36 curve, 45-degree (12015)
2	O-36 curve, 11-degree (12023)
23	O-72 curve (12041)
1	O-36 left-hand track switch (12045)
2	O-36 right-hand track switch (12046)
4	O-72 left-hand track switch (12048)
2	O-72 right-hand track switch (12049)
8	lighted bumper (12035)

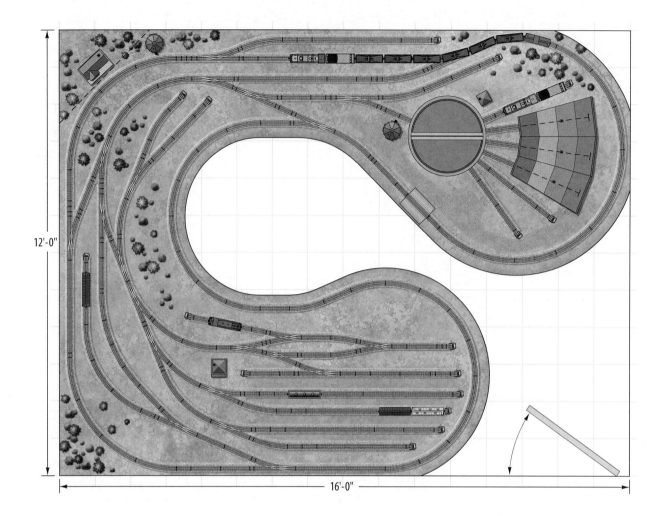

12'-0"

16'-0"

Timesaver puzzle

A basic loop of track is a simple
pleasure that nearly every toy
train operator can appreciate.
Sometimes it's the simplest
things that bring the greatest enjoyment.
But when that loop expands to include a
switching scheme of legendary status,
you've got the makings of a layout that elevates toy train operation from simple to
the sensational. That's precisely what CTT
contributor Ron Kempke accomplished
when he adapted his 12 x 16-foot O gauge
plan for continuous operation to include a
historic switching layout.

At first glance, Ron's track plan may
appear to be little more than a basic,
single-level oval design that's folded at the
center. This folded, dog-bone-shaped

scheme helps maintain a compact footprint that should fit within the walls of a
spare room or basement recreation room.
Considering that Lionel FasTrack O-60
curve sections set the minimum standard
on this plan, you wouldn't expect to find
much space left for anything else, right?
Wrong!

In a seemingly impossible transition
from simple to sensational, this plan
includes no less than a reversing loop, a
lengthy passing siding, two industrial
spurs, a four-track yard, and a locomotive servicing area with a turntable and
three-stall roundhouse. All of this is
topped off by an O gauge rendering of
John Allen's famous Timesaver switching
puzzle.

A three-rail Timesaver
John Allen was an inventive model railroader who pioneered numerous techniques and practices still used today in
model railroading. In the November 1972
issue of *Model Railroader* magazine, he
introduced a small, simple track plan
intended to turn railroad switching into a
game.

As John Allen stated, "The object of
the game is to make the required switching move in the least amount of time."
Though he gave the plan its Timesaver
moniker, that name is quite a misnomer.
It can become quite time consuming,
mentally engaging, and strangely relaxing
to work through the Timesaver switching
puzzle.

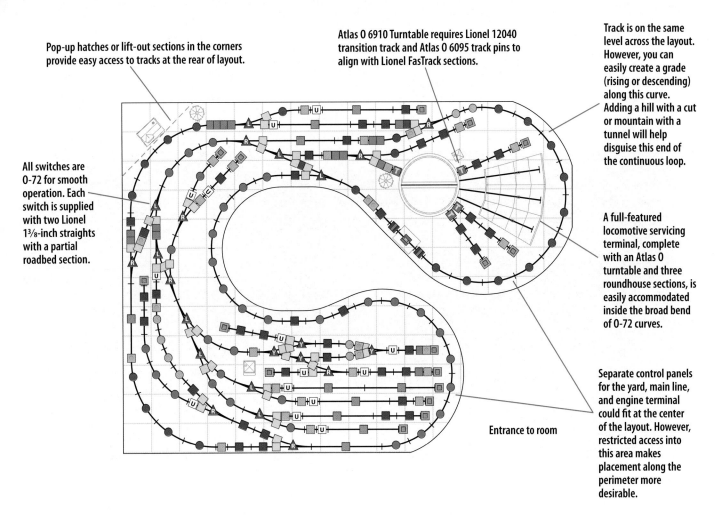

Pop-up hatches or lift-out sections in the corners provide easy access to tracks at the rear of layout.

Atlas O 6910 Turntable requires Lionel 12040 transition track and Atlas O 6095 track pins to align with Lionel FasTrack sections.

Track is on the same level across the layout. However, you can easily create a grade (rising or descending) along this curve. Adding a hill with a cut or mountain with a tunnel will help disguise this end of the continuous loop.

All switches are O-72 for smooth operation. Each switch is supplied with two Lionel 1³⁄₈-inch straights with a partial roadbed section.

A full-featured locomotive servicing terminal, complete with an Atlas O turntable and three roundhouse sections, is easily accommodated inside the broad bend of O-72 curves.

Separate control panels for the yard, main line, and engine terminal could fit at the center of the layout. However, restricted access into this area makes placement along the perimeter more desirable.

Entrance to room

If the Timesaver section of the layout isn't enough to keep you engaged, this plan also includes a small yard with four tracks used to sort cars without fouling operations on the main line. In fact, whether you're working the yard, the industrial spurs, or the Timesaver section, your switcher doesn't ever need to venture across the main line—even when moving to and from the locomotive servicing terminal.

Full-service terminal

Though it's hard to imagine, there's room for structures as large as an Atlas O operating turntable and roundhouse sections, the plan includes both of these. You'll need to use Lionel transition pieces and Atlas O transition pins to connect the FasTrack sections to the turntable. Also consider installing insulating track pins to create electrically isolated storage tracks for your prized motive power.

An operating Lionel water tower or coaling tower could provide additional intrigue when placed adjacent to the other terminal structures encircled by a ring of

O-72 curved track. If you do include more operating accessories, be sure to leave room for an access road that begins at the Lionel 12062 Grade Crossing with gates and flashers.

Working the railroad

Fitting all of these features into the 12 x 16-foot confines requires a few small concessions. The ideal location for running the layout is from a control panel at the center of the layout. Perhaps even three control panels—one for the main line, another for the terminal, and the third for the Timesaver/yard area—would be best, but access to this point is rather constricted.

The area just inside the room is a good secondary operating location, but you'll still want to create a pop-up access area at the center of the layout to reach any derailments. More likely, you'll just want a place where you can immerse yourself in all the Timesaver switching or the smooth-sailing action over the continuous mainline loop.

By Kent Johnson

LIONEL FASTRACK COMPONENTS		
Quantity	Description	Number
9	1 ³⁄₈-inch straight (12073)	
42	1 ³⁄₈-inch straight without roadbed (12074)	
16	1.75-inch straight (12026)	
2	4.5-inch straight (12025)	
19	5-inch straight (12024)	
39	10-inch straight (12014)	
10	30-inch straight (12042)	
33	O-60 curve, 22.5-degree (12056)	
22	O-72 curve, 22.5-degree (12041)	
8	O-84 curve, 11.25-degree (12061)	
4	O-72 wye track switch (12047)	
9	O-72 left-hand track switch (12048)	
9	O-72 right-hand track switch (12049)	
14	5-inch uncoupler (12020)	
2	5-inch isolated block (12029)	
4	5-inch transition (12040)	
1	grade crossing with gates and flasher (12036)	
16	bumper (12059)	

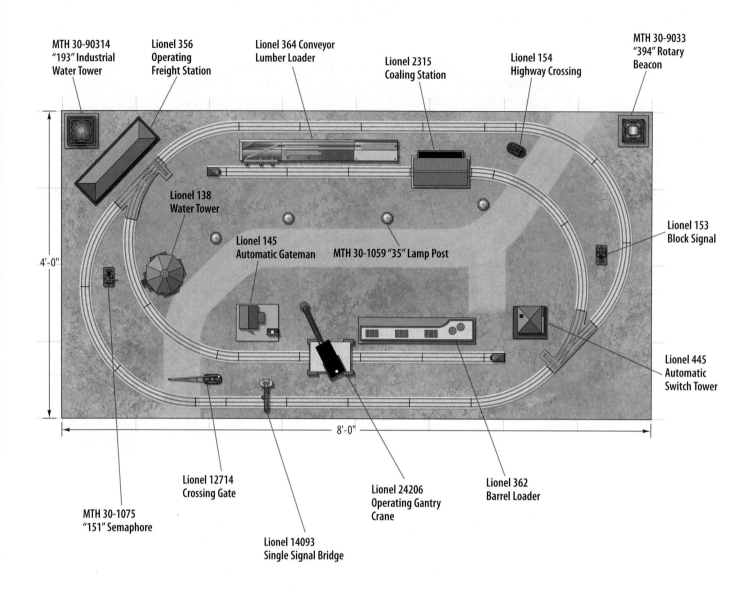

MTH 30-90314 "193" Industrial Water Tower

Lionel 356 Operating Freight Station

Lionel 364 Conveyor Lumber Loader

Lionel 2315 Coaling Station

Lionel 154 Highway Crossing

MTH 30-9033 "394" Rotary Beacon

Lionel 138 Water Tower

Lionel 145 Automatic Gateman

MTH 30-1059 "35" Lamp Post

Lionel 153 Block Signal

4'-0"

8'-0"

Lionel 445 Automatic Switch Tower

MTH 30-1075 "151" Semaphore

Lionel 12714 Crossing Gate

Lionel 14093 Single Signal Bridge

Lionel 24206 Operating Gantry Crane

Lionel 362 Barrel Loader

D-146 Dealer Display

The Ford Mustang, Chevy Camaro, and Dodge Charger are just a few of many classic American-made automobiles that have recently undergone significant reboots to include forward-thinking designs and features.

Following the lead set by these three examples, I've done the same to the 4 x 8-foot O gauge track plan for the classic Lionel D-146 dealer display.

As automakers can attest, a successful rework of a classic comes only when nos-

talgia and contemporary conveniences are balanced. My efforts to revise the original scheme for the D-146 display had to strike a balance between what worked fine on a layout in the 1950s and what works better in the 21st century.

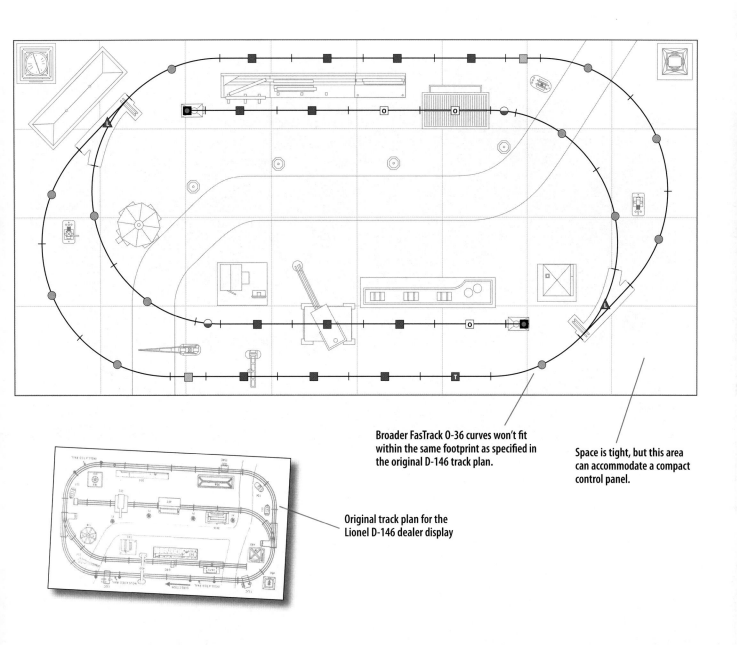

Broader FasTrack 0-36 curves won't fit within the same footprint as specified in the original D-146 track plan.

Space is tight, but this area can accommodate a compact control panel.

Original track plan for the Lionel D-146 dealer display

In developing this track plan for a *Classic Toy Trains'* project layout, I retained the traditional tubular track-work, but I shortened the length of a few sections to allow more space along the edge of the layout and substituted newer, more reliable track switches. I kept a fair number of the vintage Lionel operating accessories but swapped out others for more economical reissues produced in recent years by Lionel or MTH Electric Trains.

While continuing along this line of thinking, it occurred to me that balancing old and new was fine and dandy but not especially forward-looking. It's a bit like retooling a Dodge Charger but leaving out the HEMI.

So then, to give modelers looking to build a display-style layout with the flair and features of something more contemporary, I drafted this version of the D-146 using Lionel FasTrack components.

By Kent Johnson

LIONEL FASTRACK COMPONENTS

Quantity	Description/Number
2	5-inch straight (12024)
12	10-inch straight (12014)
12	0-36 curve, 45-degree (12015)
2	0-36 curve, 11.25-degree (12023)
2	0-36 left-hand track switch (12045)
1	terminal straight (12016)
3	operating track (12054)
2	illuminated bumper (12035)

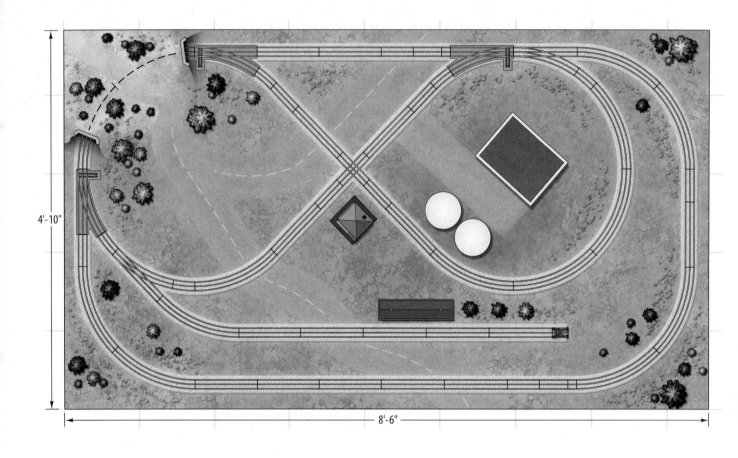

4'-10"

8'-6"

Figure Eight and More

Inserting a single crossing, a section of track that allows one line to bisect another, is one of the easiest ways to add interest to any FasTrack layout. But you don't have to stop there—especially when there's ample space to further enhance your layout's operating experience!

While this 5 x 9-foot plan maintains a basic figure-eight route at its core (Lionel 12030 add-on pack), the sections sur-

rounding this arrangement make the scheme shine.

Where trains traversing a standard figure eight can do little more than chase their tail, trains rolling over this scheme have the ability to route in reverse direction—thanks to a pair of track switches used to link the two lobes. Toss in another pair of switches, plus a few more feet of track, and you've got an extension that provides trains with a diverging main line

that routes trains away from the spiraling slapstick routine.

If that's not enough, there's still the siding located off one lobe of the figure eight. Use this to store a second locomotive, position operating cars for unloading alongside an accessory, or even a passenger train that can easily escape to the perimeter loop while another train waits its turn inside the figure eight.

By Kent Johnson

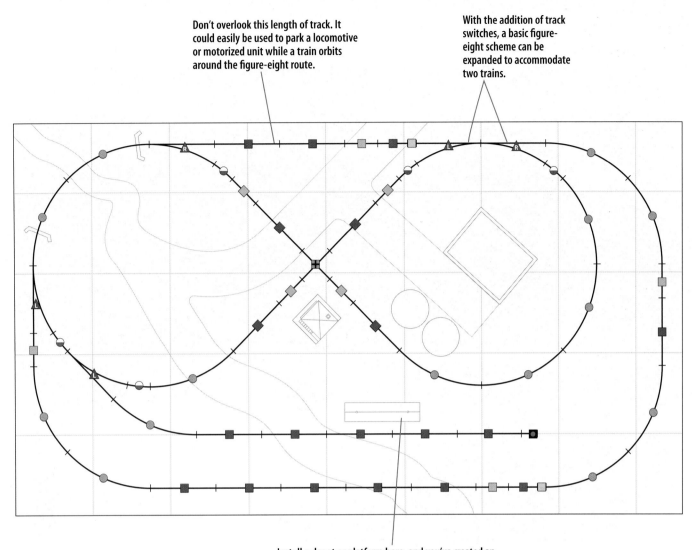

Don't overlook this length of track. It could easily be used to park a locomotive or motorized unit while a train orbits around the figure-eight route.

With the addition of track switches, a basic figure-eight scheme can be expanded to accommodate two trains.

Install a depot or platform here, and you've created an easy way to include passenger service on this layout.

LIONEL FASTRACK COMPONENTS

Quantity	Description/Number
2	1.375-inch straight (12073)
2	4.5-inch straight (12025)
8	5-inch straight (12024)
17	10-inch straight (12014)
5	0-36 curve, 11.25-degree (12023)
14	0-36 curve, 45-degree (12015)
3	0-36 left-hand track switch (12045)
2	0-36 right-hand track switch (12046)
1	90-degree crossing (12019)
1	bumper (12035)

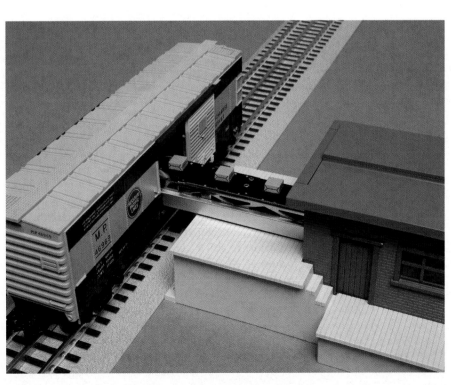

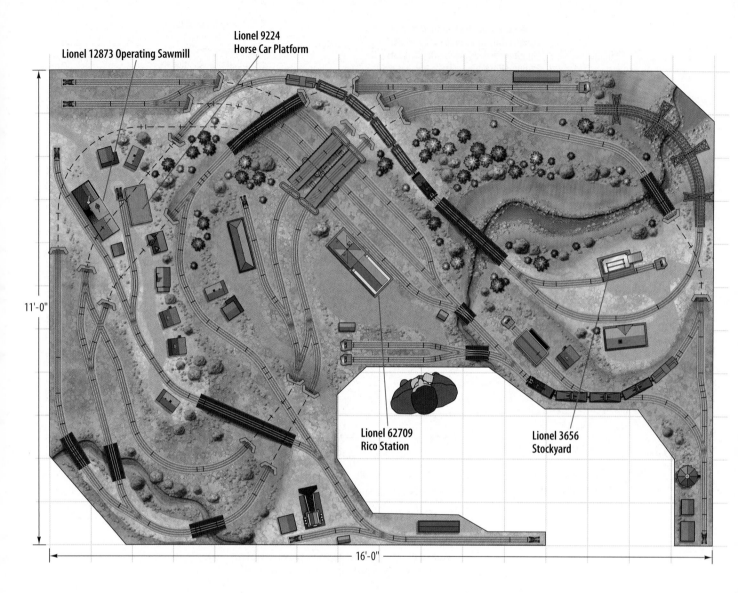

Lionel 12873 Operating Sawmill

Lionel 9224 Horse Car Platform

Lionel 62709 Rico Station

Lionel 3656 Stockyard

11'-0"

16'-0"

Rio Grande Southern

Narrow gauge railroads aren't often modeled on O gauge layouts, as our toy trains are typically able to navigate tight curves without reducing the spacing between rails. But rather than miss out on the features associated with that brand of railroading, I decided to capture many of these charms on this 11 x 16-foot O gauge track plan.

My version of a western narrow gauge railroad was inspired by a scheme from the late John Armstrong, an innovative contributor to *Model Railroader* magazine. I adapted his original HO scale plan for the Rio Grande Southern, a railroad

serving the silver mining towns in the mountains of western Colorado well into the 1950s, to suit Lionel O gauge FasTrack components.

To represent an appropriate mountain railroad setting, I made generous use of noticeable grades (as much as 4 percent), tight curves (O-36 minimum), and smaller-portioned equipment and structures. The selectively compressed (O-27) locomotives and rolling stock are good options. Structures on this layout are generally associated with the cattle ranching, logging, and mining industries, each of which provides good reason to include operating accessories and freight cars.

The real draw of this layout is the potential for spectacular western mountain scenery. Rail lines are carved out of sheer cliffs and route through numerous tunnels and over tall trestles crossing steep gorges, tumbling rapids, and waterfalls. Depending on the type of mountain range you model, it's possible to get by without adding a large number of trees. The goal is to develop terrain that looks as though it can challenge our toy trains.

While this may not be the route of the *Super Chief*, tiny trains slowly negotiating precarious mountain tracks can be every bit as exciting!

By Michael Tylick

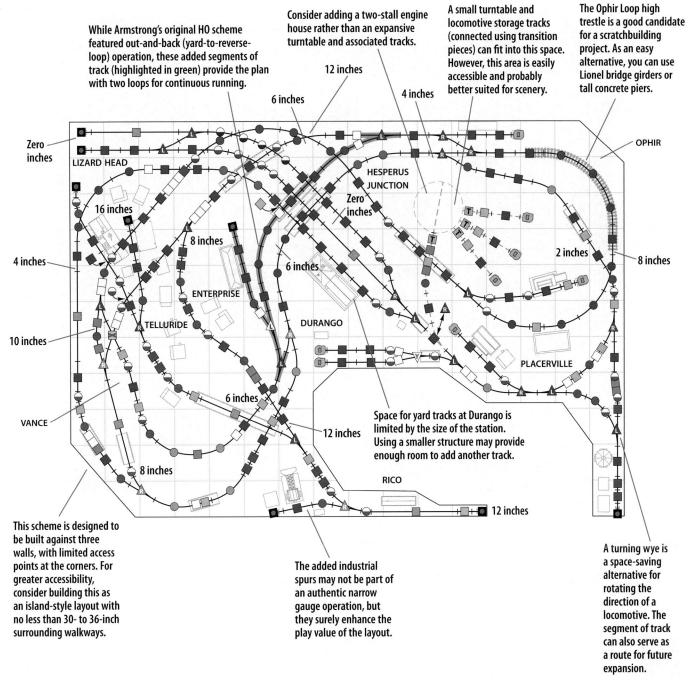

While Armstrong's original HO scheme featured out-and-back (yard-to-reverse-loop) operation, these added segments of track (highlighted in green) provide the plan with two loops for continuous running.

Consider adding a two-stall engine house rather than an expansive turntable and associated tracks.

A small turntable and locomotive storage tracks (connected using transition pieces) can fit into this space. However, this area is easily accessible and probably better suited for scenery.

The Ophir Loop high trestle is a good candidate for a scratchbuilding project. As an easy alternative, you can use Lionel bridge girders or tall concrete piers.

12 inches

6 inches

4 inches

Zero inches

LIZARD HEAD

OPHIR

HESPERUS JUNCTION

Zero inches

16 inches

8 inches

4 inches

ENTERPRISE

6 inches

2 inches

8 inches

10 inches

TELLURIDE

DURANGO

PLACERVILLE

VANCE

6 inches

12 inches

Space for yard tracks at Durango is limited by the size of the station. Using a smaller structure may provide enough room to add another track.

8 inches

RICO

12 inches

This scheme is designed to be built against three walls, with limited access points at the corners. For greater accessibility, consider building this as an island-style layout with no less than 30- to 36-inch surrounding walkways.

The added industrial spurs may not be part of an authentic narrow gauge operation, but they surely enhance the play value of the layout.

A turning wye is a space-saving alternative for rotating the direction of a locomotive. The segment of track can also serve as a route for future expansion.

LIONEL FASTRACK COMPONENTS

Quantity		Description/Number
26	☐	1.375-inch straight (12073)
10	◼	1.75-inch straight (12026)
15	◼	4.5-inch straight (12025)
20	◻	5-inch straight (12024)
78	◼	10-inch straight (12014)
6	◼	30-inch straight (12042)
28	◡	0-36 curve, 11.25-degree (12023)
22	●	0-36 curve, 22.5-degree (12022)
7	○	0-36 curve, 45-degree (12015)
14	●	0-48 curve, 30-degree (12043)
4	●	0-60 curve, 22.5-degree (12056)
8	◡	0-72 curve, 11.25-degree (12055)

Quantity		Description/Number
6	●	0-72 curve, 22.5-degree (12041)
4	◡	0-84 curve, 11.25-degree (12061)
4	△	0-36 right-hand track switch, manual (12018)
11	▲	0-36 left-hand track switch (12045)
8	▲	0-36 right-hand track switch (12046)
1	△	0-60 left-hand track switch (12057)
1	▲	0-72 left-hand track switch (12048)
1	▽	0-72 wye switch (12047)
4	T	5-inch transition straight (12040)
1	⊠	45-degree crossing (12051)
8	▣	bumper (12059)
8	◼	lighted bumper (12035)

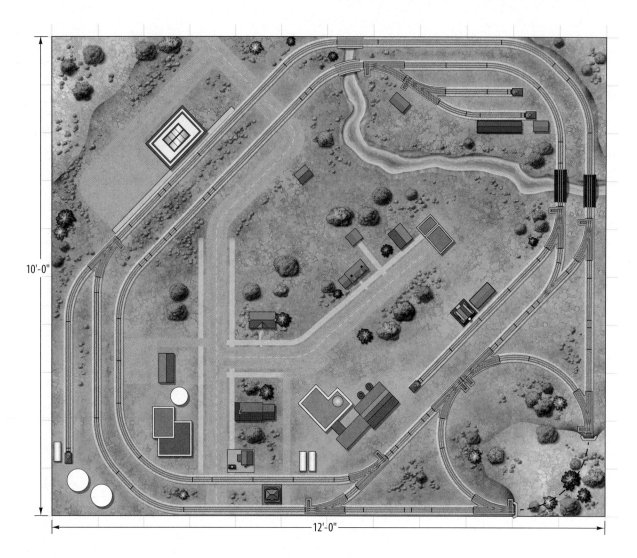

10'-0"

12'-0"

Reversing Circle

Here's a 10 x 12-foot track plan taken from Lionel's *Handbook for Model Railroaders* from 1940 but redrawn with Lionel's new FasTrack.

Lionel's plan uses traditional tubular track and O-31 curves and switches. This version follows the original's design but uses broader FasTrack O-36 curves and switches.

Two trains and a reverse circle

This track plan lets you operate two trains hands free, each in a clockwise or a counterclockwise direction. If you divide each of the loops into two electrical blocks (allowing you to temporarily park a train on one half of the loop by toggling off the power while a second train enters or leaves the other half of the loop), you'll be

able to move trains from the inner loop to the outer loop and vice-versa.

That's not a new concept, but what may be new to you is the way this track plan uses a circle of track, nestled in one corner of the layout, to allow trains to reverse direction. If you follow a train clockwise along the outer loop, it can use the circle to reverse itself and travel counterclockwise on the outer loop or inner loop.

Trains running on the inner loop also can use the circle to reverse direction. To rejoin the inner loop, they need to make one circuit around the outer loop and then take the diverging route of a track switch to rejoin the inner loop. Spend a few moments tracing your finger around the track plan in clockwise and counterclockwise directions and you'll see what I mean.

Using Lionel FasTrack

On the FasTrack plan, I've drawn the four spur tracks as depicted in the original diagram. If I were to build this layout, I'd rearrange them for more length.

You'll see many small straight sections of FasTrack on the track plan, particularly along the approaches to the circle. Lionel offers FasTrack straight sections in lengths of 30, 10, 5, 4.5, and 1.75 inches. FasTrack cannot easily be cut like tubular track without regard to electrical connections, so to adapt the 1940 plan to FasTrack requires the use of nearly two dozen 1.75 fitter sections.

All the curves are O-36, and I used 45-degree, 22.5-degree, and 11.25-degree sections.

The track switches are O-36 remote-control switches. Lionel catalogs its

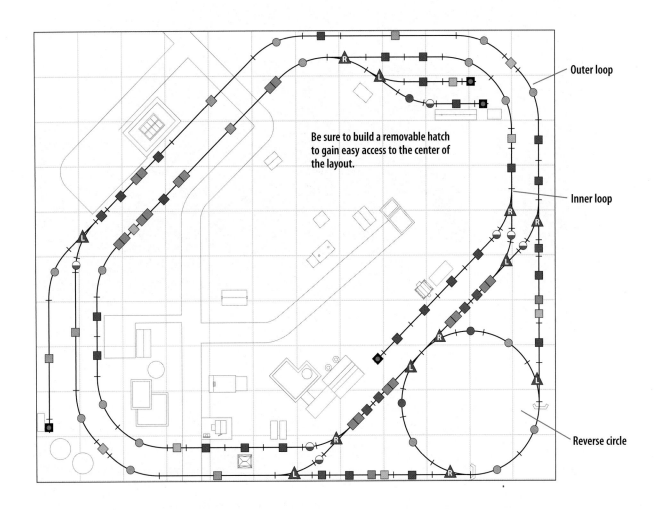

Be sure to build a removable hatch to gain easy access to the center of the layout.

Outer loop

Inner loop

Reverse circle

remote-control O-36 switches with a separate quarter-curve section to complete a 45-degree turn. Only seven of these quarter curves are required to build this layout, so you'll be able to substitute four of the leftover quarter curves for two of the half curves specified in the list of track components.

Scenery and suggestions

On the two-dimensional track plan, the circle may look odd. But you'll see in the illustration that a quarter of the circle is hidden inside a tunnel. This small scenery trick goes a long way toward making the circle look more presentable if your goal is greater realism.

Typical of prewar and postwar track plans, there's a lot of empty real estate beyond arm's reach in the center. If I were building this O gauge layout today, I'd

either make a removable hatch in the center or leave the middle open and construct a hinged lift-up section to gain access.

Given when this track plan was originally designed, it's no surprise that the key accessories on this layout are all prewar Lionel: 98 Coal Bunker, 115 City Station, and 438 Signal Tower. Also on the drawing are a 93 Water Tower, 156 Station Platform, 440N Signal Bridge, two 46 Crossing

Gates, and several 060 Telegraph Poles. All can be replaced with postwar or current pieces from any manufacturer.

Back in 1940, much of the town in the center of the layout would have been scratchbuilt. Today, it can easily be constructed from seemingly dozens of residential and commercial structures.

There you have it, a classic O gauge plan from the 1940s updated to the 21st century.

By Neil Besougloff

LIONEL FASTRACK COMPONENTS		
Quantity	Description/Number	
6	30-inch straight (12042)	16 ⬤ 0-36 45-degree curve (12015)
24	10-inch straight (12014)	3 ⬤ 0-36 22.5-degree curve (12022)
8	5-inch straight (12024)	7 ◖ 0-36 11.25-degree curve (12023)
7	4.5-inch straight (12025)	6 ⚠ 0-36 remote-control left-hand switch (12045)
20	1.75-inch straight (12026)	6 ⚠ 0-36 remote-control right-hand switch (12046)
		4 ⬛ bumper (12059)

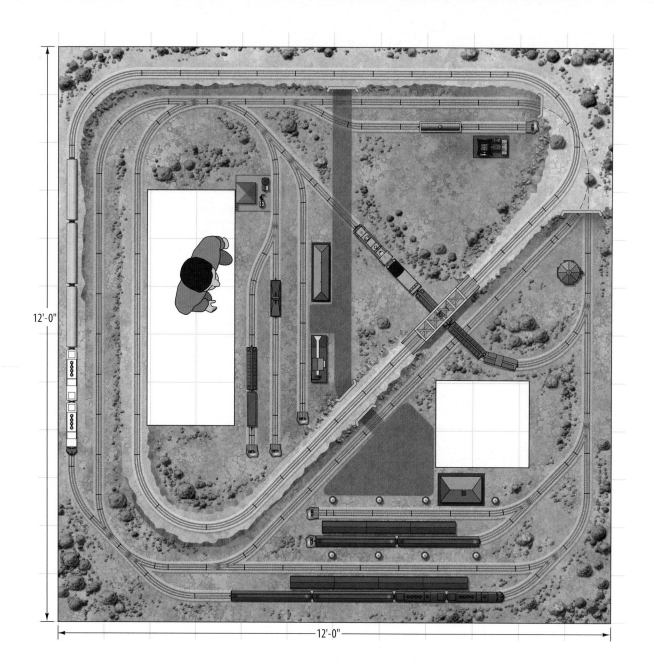

12'-0"

12'-0"

Scenic Limited

Of the many layout plans the Lionel Corp. published, the most familiar are probably the table layout schemes from the 1950s. There's another important group of Lionel plans, however, and they are very different. Look back at the O gauge trains of the early 1940s, and you'll find prewar scale and scale-detailed locomotives. At that point in its history, Lionel was betting that the future of O gauge trains lay in the direction of increasing realism.

With that in mind, it's no surprise many of the Lionel track plans of this period had the characteristics associated with today's realism-oriented designs. These traits include long mainline runs and even around-the-walls schemes.

Updating the Scenic Limited
This plan is a modern update of the Scenic Limited scheme first featured in *Model Builder* magazine. My version splits the difference between the two previously

mentioned styles to combine traditional table layout construction with a more open design. It's a mid-sized layout—just less than 150 square feet—and the construction is simple. At the same time, it includes a good-sized passenger station, up-and-over operation, a small freight yard, along with multiple routes.

Schematically, the layout is a large oval with two alternate routes plus a reversing loop. The first alternate route is the freight cutoff, which keeps freight trains out of

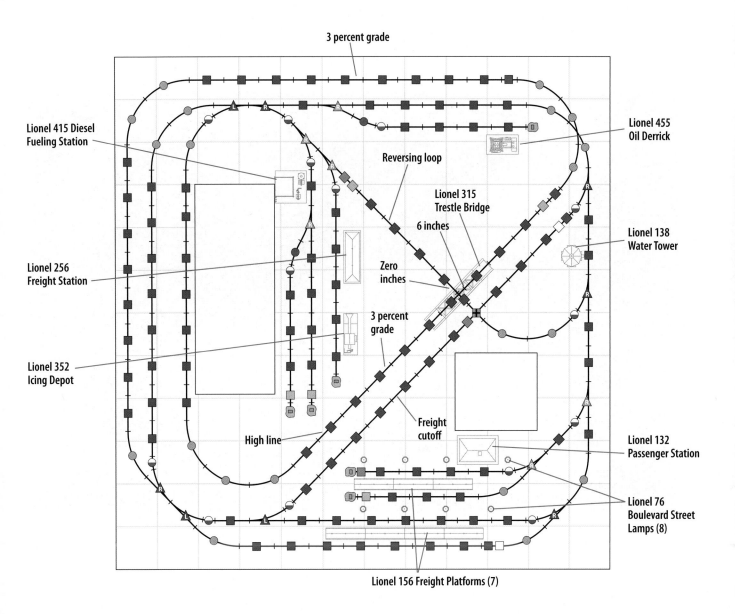

Lionel 415 Diesel Fueling Station

Lionel 256 Freight Station

Lionel 352 Icing Depot

3 percent grade

Reversing loop

Lionel 315 Trestle Bridge

6 inches

Zero inches

3 percent grade

High line

Freight cutoff

Lionel 455 Oil Derrick

Lionel 138 Water Tower

Lionel 132 Passenger Station

Lionel 76 Boulevard Street Lamps (8)

Lionel 156 Freight Platforms (7)

the passenger station. The second alternate route is the high line that goes up and over both the main line and the reversing loop, creating an interesting juxtaposition of a bridge with a 90-degree crossing.

Adding the trains

Trains arrive and depart from both a passenger station and a small freight yard. Several operating accessories, including an icing depot, add interest to the yard. Express refrigerator cars arriving at the passenger station will need to go over to the freight yard to be iced, and passenger diesels will likewise need to go to the yard for fuel.

With enough trackage to hold three trains comfortably, this layout is suited for command control, although cab control will work also. It isn't well suited for the "one transformer per loop" style of wiring, however. I've drawn the plan to include two access areas: one that remains open and a parking lot that doubles as a hatch.

As I picture this layout, I imagine a Berkshire steamer leading a freight on the high line while a pair of New York Central F3 diesels pulls into the passenger station and a switcher works the yard. Whether you use these locomotives or your own favorites, one thing is certain—this layout will be as much fun to operate today as it was for those 1940s Lionel railroaders fortunate enough to build it the first time it was published.

By Terry Thompson

LIONEL FASTRACK COMPONENTS

Quantity	Description/Number
2	☐ 1.375-inch straight (12073)
3	▨ 1.75-inch straight (12026)
5	■ 4.5-inch straight (12025)
5	▢ 5-inch straight (12024)
107	■ 10-inch straight (12014)
14	◠ 0-36 11.25-degree curve (12023)
2	● 0-36 22.5-degree curve (12022)
20	● 0-36 45-degree curve (12015)
3	△ 0-36 left-hand remote switch (12045)
6	△ 0-36 right-hand manual switch (12018)
5	△ 0-36 right-hand remote switch (12046)
1	✛ 90-degree crossing (12019)
6	▣ bumper (12059)

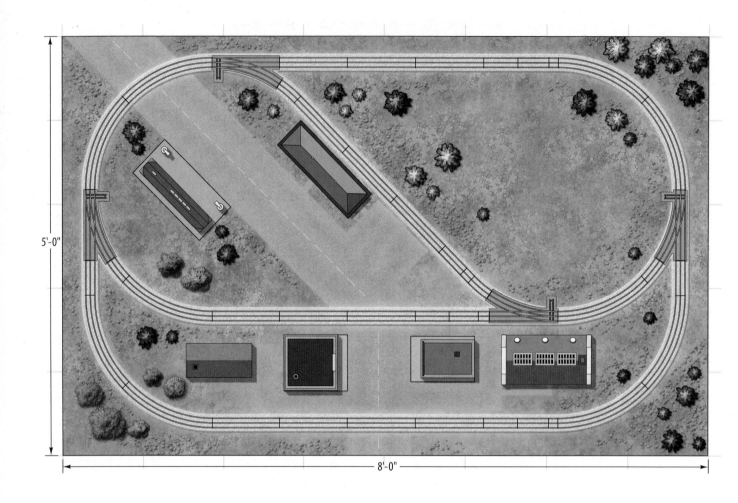

5'-0"

8'-0"

Needmore Ry.

What do you do when a 4 x 8 footprint no longer accommodates all you desire from a toy train layout? You add on! Fortunately, an expansion doesn't need to be extensive in order to be effective. By extending a 4-foot leg by just one foot, the resulting 5 x 8-foot area makes room for a reverse loop and passing siding.

It is easy to extend a sheet of plywood by using screws to attach (evenly spaced) three lengths of 1 x 3 dimensional lumber to the underside and securing a 1 x 8 cut strip of plywood. Some home improvement centers can cut plywood right in the store, so you don't have to worry about transporting a full sheet or having to have a circular saw on hand.

With this extended footprint comes the extra bit of width needed to add a passing siding to a basic oval with a reverse loop. And after adding the passing siding, you'll still have room to squeeze in a small yard by installing a few track switches either along the reverse loop cutoff or on a curve on the original oval configuration.

By Kent Johnson

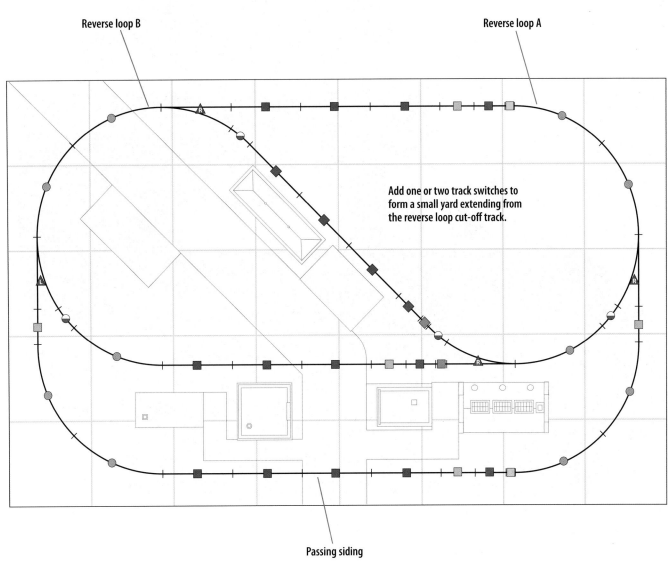

Reverse loop B

Reverse loop A

Add one or two track switches to form a small yard extending from the reverse loop cut-off track.

Passing siding

LIONEL FASTRACK COMPONENTS

Quantity	Description/Number
2	1.375-inch straight (12073)
2	1.75-inch straight (12026)
4	4.5-inch straight (12025)
5	5-inch straight (12024)
13	10-inch straight (12014)
4	0-36 curve, 11.25-degree (12023)
10	0-36 curve, 45-degree (12015)
1	0-36 left-hand track switch (12045)
3	0-36 right-hand track switch (12046)

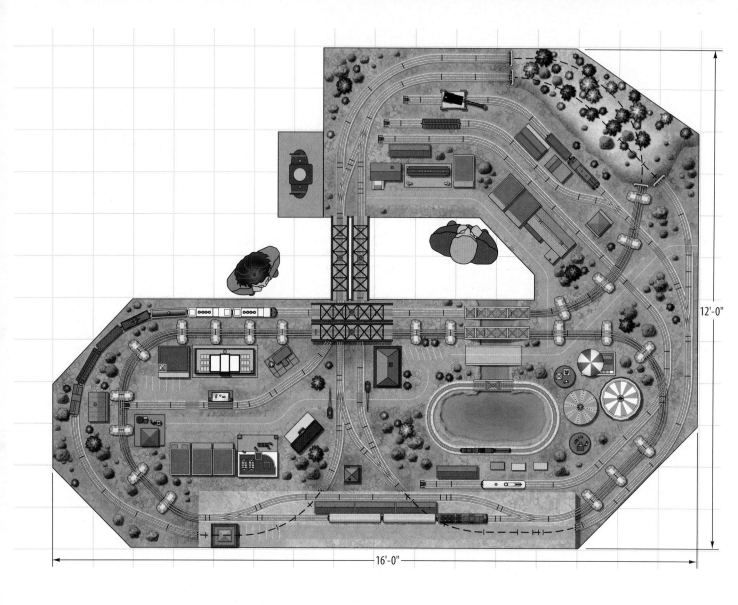

12'-0"

16'-0"

Three Loop Railroad

Mario DiFede designed this action-packed track plan to simultaneously run three trains over three loops of Lionel FasTrack.

According to Mario: My underlying objective was to design an all-Lionel layout that included plenty of action both on and off the rails. At the core of the layout, you'll find one over/under figure-eight loop of track and another oval loop that are connected by two pairs of Fas-Track 12057 and 12058 O-60 track switches. These loops primarily use 12056

O-60 curves to accommodate scale-length locomotives operated under command control.

A third loop, elevated by 12038 Fas-Track trestles, is intended for passenger or commuter trains operating under conventional transformer operation. In addition to this elevated route, I've included a point-to-point line that hosts a trolley. Just when you think there's no more room for another train, I've added a loop of N scale track to model a miniature ride-on train for the kids gathered at the carnival grounds.

Accessory action

Beyond the track, I've separated the layout into three areas. Within one loop I've established a downtown scene. In one of the remaining two loops, you'll find an industrial complex. Then in the last loop, there's plenty of space for a carnival and all the rides and attractions associated with the festivities.

Ranging from a full-action portal gantry crane to a spinning carousel, there are nearly two dozen Lionel operating accessories on the layout that keep pace with the action on the rails.

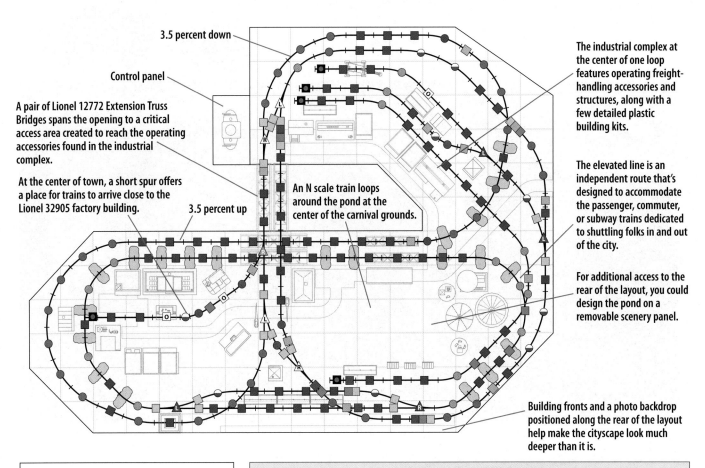

3.5 percent down

Control panel

A pair of Lionel 12772 Extension Truss Bridges spans the opening to a critical access area created to reach the operating accessories found in the industrial complex.

At the center of town, a short spur offers a place for trains to arrive close to the Lionel 32905 factory building.

3.5 percent up

An N scale train loops around the pond at the center of the carnival grounds.

The industrial complex at the center of one loop features operating freight-handling accessories and structures, along with a few detailed plastic building kits.

The elevated line is an independent route that's designed to accommodate the passenger, commuter, or subway trains dedicated to shuttling folks in and out of the city.

For additional access to the rear of the layout, you could design the pond on a removable scenery panel.

Building fronts and a photo backdrop positioned along the rear of the layout help make the cityscape look much deeper than it is.

LIONEL FASTRACK COMPONENTS

Quantity	Description/Number
21	1.375-inch fitter (12073)
9	1.75-inch straight (12026)
7	4.5-inch straight (12025)
12	5-inch straight (12024)
81	10-inch straight (12014)
15	O-36 curve, 45-degree (12015)
5	O-36 curve, 22.5-degree (12022)
2	O-36 curve, 11.25-degree (12023)
1	O-48 curve, 30-degree (12043)
29	O-60 curve, 22.5-degree (12056)
7	O-72 curve, 22.5-degree (12041)
1	O-72 curve, 11.25-degree (12055)
1	O-36 left-hand switch (12045)
1	O-36 manual right-hand switch (12018)
2	O-60 left-hand switch (12057)
2	O-60 right-hand switch (12058)
2	O-72 left-hand switch (12048)
1	O-72 right-hand switch (12049)
5	lighted bumper (12035)
21	trestles (12038)
3	operating track (12054)

SUGGESTED ACCESSORIES

Lionel Number	Product	Number	Product
2152	Crossing gate (2)	14170	Swing ride
2315	Coaling station	14231	Cotton candy booth
2319	Watch tower	22915	Municipal building
2324	Operating switch tower	22933	Section gang shed
9220	Milk car platform	24161	Test O' Strength
12701	Fueling station	24172	Balancing man
12770	Arch-under bridge (2)	24176	Irene's Diner
12772	Extension truss bridge (4)	24177	Hot air balloon ride
12802	Lighted roadside diner	24182	Fire station
12818	Animated freight station	24183	Gas station
12905	Factory	32905	Lionel factory
12943	Station platform (5)	34126	Market
12961	Newsstand with diesel horn	34127	O'Grady's Tavern
14109	Carousel	34128	Pharmacy
14134	"282" magnet crane	34129	Kiddie City Toys
14152	"133" station	34130	Five and Ten
14160	Hotdog stand	34131	Al's Hardware
14161	Hobo shack	34159	Camel ride stand

Adding scenery and access

It's hard to believe, but even with these components compressed into an 12 x 16 space, there's room for scenery and the ever-important access points required for resetting accessories or rerailing a wayward train. You can easily add a hidden pop-up hatch at the center of the carnival grounds.

Installing space-saving photo backdrops along the back and/or sides of the layout keeps scenery clutter to a minimum and provides the illusion that there's more depth to the layout, especially the city scenes.

Most likely, layout visitors will be too enthralled with the fast-paced FasTrack action to pay much attention to the simple scenery!

By Mario DiFede and Kent Johnson

4'-0"

8'-0"

Cascade & Timber Trail

T he mental challenge of developing a suitable track plan is often cited as an obstacle to building a permanent toy train layout. Another common reason for avoiding the construction of a fun-filled railroad is the false notion that it requires an inordinate amount of time to develop, specialized construction skills, and hard-to-find products.

"Nonsense," is what we think you'll say to that—especially after examining our scheme for a logging-themed 4 x 8-foot O gauge layout named the Cascade & Timber Trail Ry.

With the creation of this track plan, the *Classic Toy Trains* magazine staff set out to dispel most of the myths about designing and building an enjoyable toy train layout of any size. Regarding the size of the layout, we decided to restrict the plan to the smallest common layout dimension— 4 x 8 feet. We sought to prove that you can easily fit plenty of railroad and realistic scenery atop a single sheet of uncut plywood or foam insulation board.

Speaking of construction materials, we also thought it was important that the plan feature readily available materials and products. If it wasn't likely that you could find a particular item at your local hobby shop or home improvement center, we simply didn't include it in the plan. Additionally, these products needed to be safe and easy to use, without the need for expensive power tools.

Cascade Range logging set

Of all toy train products, perhaps the easiest to use is a train set that comes complete with reliable trains, track, and a transformer. That's why we elected to shape this plan around the Lionel Cascade Range Logging set (30021). [Although no longer manufactured, the set can be found online, or you can use similar individual components.]

The set comes with a generous 40" x 60" loop of FasTrack. While much of the track provided in the set can be used to assemble the track plan, you still need to purchase additional track sections to complete the railway.

Track assembly

First, we identified each track section required in the plan. Then, starting in a corner of the layout, we laid two straight

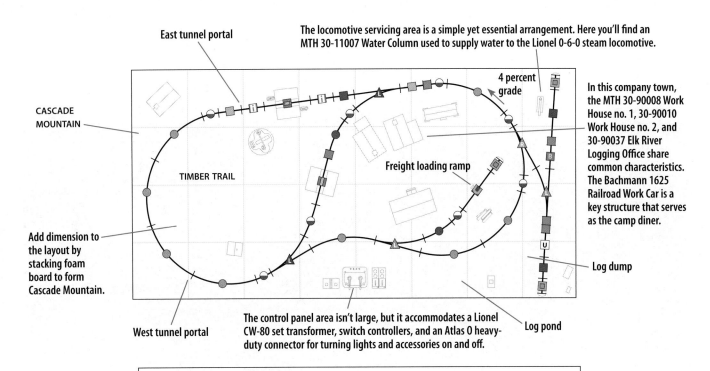

East tunnel portal

The locomotive servicing area is a simple yet essential arrangement. Here you'll find an MTH 30-11007 Water Column used to supply water to the Lionel 0-6-0 steam locomotive.

CASCADE MOUNTAIN

4 percent grade

In this company town, the MTH 30-90008 Work House no. 1, 30-90010 Work House no. 2, and 30-90037 Elk River Logging Office share common characteristics. The Bachmann 1625 Railroad Work Car is a key structure that serves as the camp diner.

TIMBER TRAIL

Freight loading ramp

Add dimension to the layout by stacking foam board to form Cascade Mountain.

Log dump

West tunnel portal

The control panel area isn't large, but it accommodates a Lionel CW-80 set transformer, switch controllers, and an Atlas O heavy-duty connector for turning lights and accessories on and off.

Log pond

LIONEL FASTRACK COMPONENTS

Quantity	Description/Number		Quantity	Description/Number
5	1.75-inch straight (12026)		1	0-36 manual right-hand turnout (12018)
2	4.5-inch straight (12025)		2	0-36 remote left-hand turnout (12045)
2	5-inch straight (12024)		1	5-inch uncoupler (12020)
1	10-inch straight (12014)		2	5-inch isolator (12029)
7	0-36 curve, 11.25-degree (12023)		1	5-inch block section (12060)
2	0-36 curve, 22.5-degree (12022)		1	10-inch terminal straight (12016)
8	0-36 curve, 45-degree (12015)		1	grade crossing (12036)
1	0-72 curve, 11.25-degree (12055)		1	grade crossing with flashers (12062)
2	0-36 manual left-hand turnout (12017)		3	track bumper (12059)

sections on a flat surface and pushed them firmly together. Curved sections and switches go together the same way to form a complete loop of track around the entire layout.

Just as on real railroads, it's very important to create a stable surface for your toy train trackwork. Although Lionel FasTrack and other contemporary track found in train sets features sturdy, hard plastic roadbed, we installed Woodland Scenics Track-Bed (ST1476) under all our sections, including switches and grade crossings. This flexible, soft foam material quiets track noise, smooths irregularities along the risers and inclines, and shapes a realistic track profile.

Install foam tabletop

On our Cascade & Timber Trail Ry., we installed a ½" x 6" multi-density fiber-board (MDF) border around the layout edges. This border, or fascia, keeps the foam in place, but you can also use foam-compatible adhesive to permanently

attach the board. Additionally, the MDF border protects the soft foam edges from damage.

With the foam tabletop in place, you're ready to test-fit the track plan. At this point, many layout builders gather up and loosely assemble all the required track, switches, and accessories. Instead, we used our computer-generated track plan to perform a virtual test-fit of these layout components. By printing out a full-scale (1" = 1") version of our plan, we could easily identify and modify issues regarding placement without having all the layout components on hand. You can download the full-scale plan at ctt.trains.com/operating/how to/2011/05/all about the cascade and timber trail ry.aspx.

By Kent Johnson

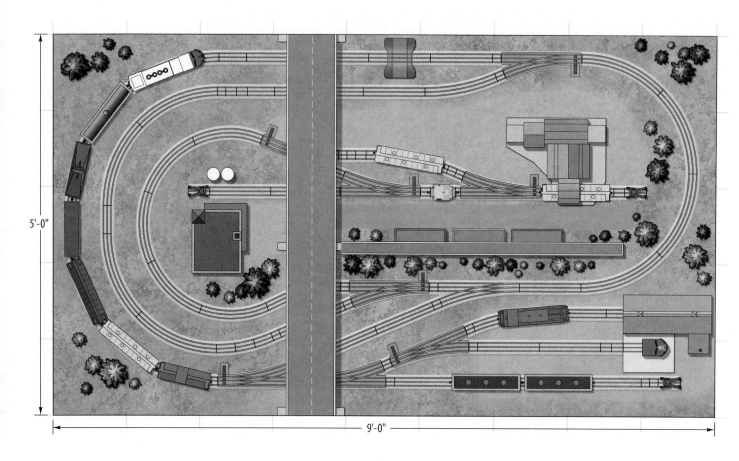

5'-0"

9'-0"

Red Wing Ry.

Until recently, I would have run away screaming had someone asked me to design a small O gauge layout that featured continuous mainline running, wide-radius track switches, a passing siding, a compact freight yard with an engine servicing area, and a dedicated industrial switching site. But that was before I discovered a little gem lurking in the Lionel FasTrack product line. While the 36-inch-diameter curved section has served as the standard (minimum) from the start, Lionel's recent introduction of the 37103 31-inch-diameter curve now makes the impossible very possible.

As evident in this 5 x 9-foot plan, the latest FasTrack O-31 curved section gives

layout builders reason for celebration, as it's now practical to include multiple loops of track in a compact area. Truth be told, physical attributes (the width of the molded-plastic roadbed) of FasTrack prevents builders from forming truly concentric curves using O-31 and standard O-36 curves. However, adding just a single straight fitter section at the top of the wider O-36 curve makes it practical to include two or even three nested loops of track on a small layout.

A plan filled with features

At one end of this track plan, my adaptation of a *Model Railroader* magazine HO scale project layout, you'll see adjacent

O-31, O-36, and O-48 FasTrack curves. Moving from the inner to outer tracks, this arrangement represents curved routes along an industrial branch line, a passing siding, and a wide-sweeping main line. On a layout with limited space, you're lucky to have one, let alone all three, of these design features. That's the benefit of starting with a tight yet serviceable O-31 curved section.

Other "big layout" features fit to this limited space include FasTrack O-60 remote-controlled switches. At nearly half the curvature of an O-36 switch, these broad switches keep scale-proportion locomotives and rolling stock from navigating neck-breaking moves through the freight yard and industrial area.

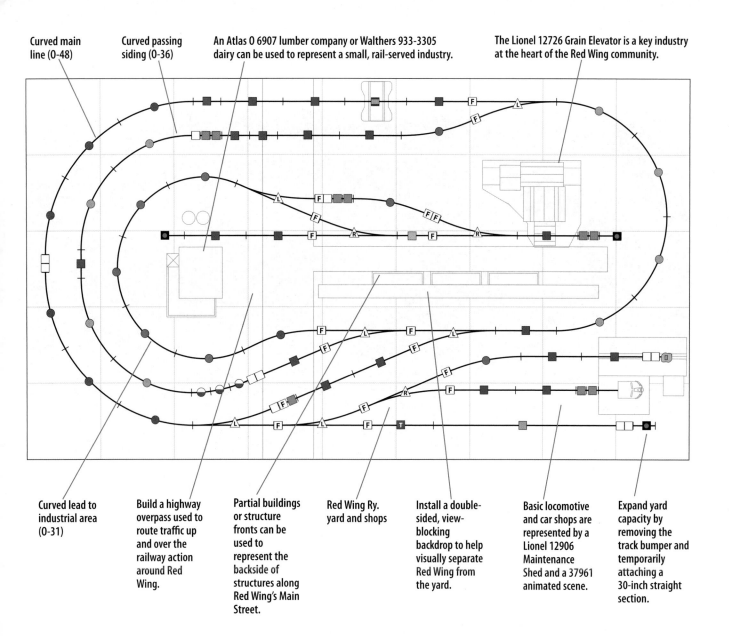

Curved main line (0-48)

Curved passing siding (0-36)

An Atlas O 6907 lumber company or Walthers 933-3305 dairy can be used to represent a small, rail-served industry.

The Lionel 12726 Grain Elevator is a key industry at the heart of the Red Wing community.

Curved lead to industrial area (0-31)

Build a highway overpass used to route traffic up and over the railway action around Red Wing.

Partial buildings or structure fronts can be used to represent the backside of structures along Red Wing's Main Street.

Red Wing Ry. yard and shops

Install a double-sided, view-blocking backdrop to help visually separate Red Wing from the yard.

Basic locomotive and car shops are represented by a Lionel 12906 Maintenance Shed and a 37961 animated scene.

Expand yard capacity by removing the track bumper and temporarily attaching a 30-inch straight section.

That's right, this 5 x 9-foot layout also features a three-track yard with locomotive maintenance facilities. You don't need a lot of space to store a few freight cars destined for the industrial branch, but you can easily increase the capacity by adding sections at the end of Yard Track no. 1.

Running trains

At the center of the industrial switching area, I've included a runaround track. This short but essential arrangement permits a small switcher or an even smaller Lionel Trackmobile motorized unit to pull or push cars into place at the two industries. Even with just two industries, the work of positioning cars before, after, and

during loading and unloading is enough to keep a layout operator busy while another operator keeps a train rolling along the main line.

And when it comes to running trains on this 5 x 9 plan, a Lionel Legacy command control system seems in order to handle the three possible operating positions. You'll want one remote to run and route the mainline train, while another operator handles duties in the industrial area and yard. As you can see, there's plenty to do on this small railroad.

By Kent Johnson

LIONEL FASTRACK COMPONENTS

Quantity		Description/Number
18	F	1.375-inch straight fitter (12000X)
11	☐	1.375-inch straight (12073)
9	▣	1.75-inch straight (12026)
4	■	4.5-inch straight (12025)
1	▣	5-inch straight (12024)
16	■	10-inch straight (12014)
1	T	10-inch terminal straight (12016)
1	▣	30-inch straight (12042)
5	●	0-31 curve, 45-degree (37103)
8	●	0-36 curve, 45-degree (12015)
3	◡	0-48 curve, 7.5-degree (16835)
7	●	0-48 curve, 30-degree (12043)
3	●	0-60 curve, 22.5-degree (12056)
6	⚠	0-60 left-hand remote switch (12057)
3	⚠	0-60 right-hand remote switch (12058)
1	▦	grade crossing (12036)
3	■	lighted bumper (12035)
1	▣	earthen bumper (12059)

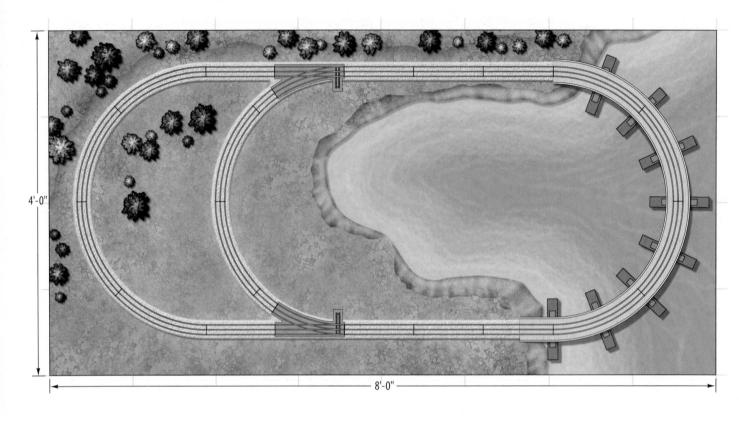

4'-0"

8'-0"

Loop Line

Standard 36-inch FasTrack curves fit nicely within the dimension of a 4 x 8-foot sheet of plywood, while leaving some extra space for scenery, signals, and accessories at the perimeter. Just about the only thing you can't fit along the outer perimeter is another loop of track. But what about the space inside the oval?

In this scheme, adding a pair of track switches at one end of the oval makes it possible to include a curved passing siding without expanding the original 4 x 8 footprint.

At the opposite end of the oval, there's plenty of room to insert a track switch or two and form a small yard, also inside the loop. However, if you do have bigger plans

for expansion, then simply add another sheet of plywood to form an L-shaped railroad that fits nicely into a corner.

For a more unique layout, you can set the railroad along a river inlet. Build one end of the loop into the water on piers, add some quaint buildings, and you have the makings of a fun-filled tourist railroad.

By Kent Johnson

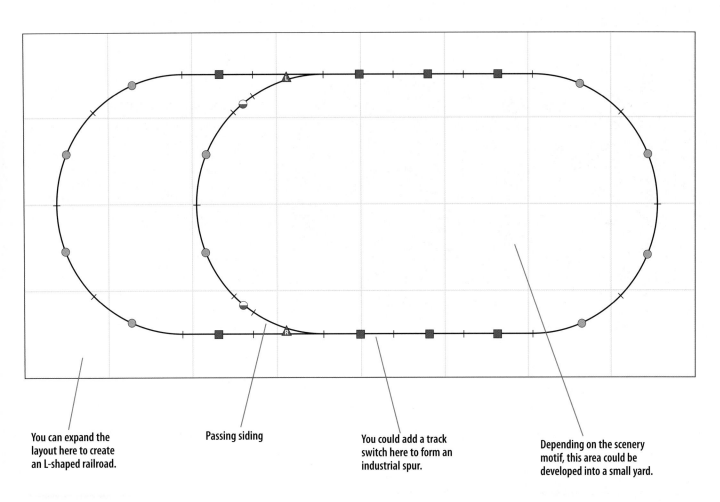

You can expand the
layout here to create
an L-shaped railroad.

Passing siding

You could add a track
switch here to form an
industrial spur.

Depending on the scenery
motif, this area could be
developed into a small yard.

LIONEL FASTRACK COMPONENTS

Quantity	Description/Number
8	■ 10-inch straight (12014)
2	◖ 0-36 curve, 11.25-degree (12023)
10	● 0-36 curve, 45-degree (12015)
1	▲ 0-36 left-hand track switch (12045)
1	▲ᴿ 0-36 right-hand track switch (12046)

Model trains have been a part of Christmas almost since the first one (model train, not Christmas). Putting a train under a tree often adds the finishing touch to the season's display. To make your Christmas jollier, we have included three FasTrack layouts that you can easily put under your tree.

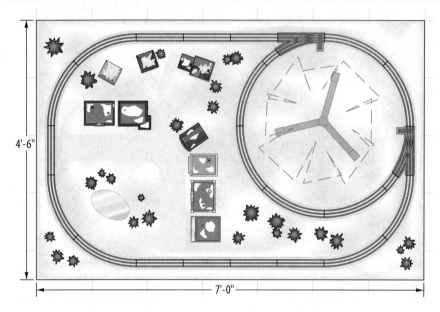

LIONEL FASTRACK COMPONENTS	
Quantity	Description/Number
8	10-inch straight (12014)
2	O-36 curve, 11.25-degree (12023)
12	O-36 curve, 45-degree (12015)
1	O-36 left-hand track switch (12045)
1	O-36 right-hand track switch (12046)

4'-6"

7'-0"

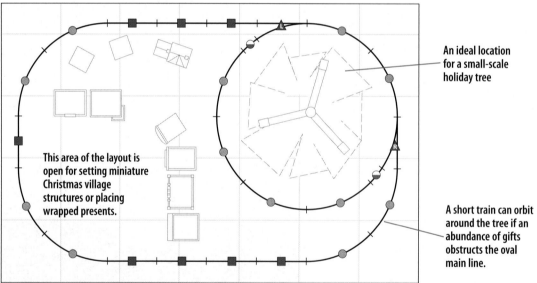

An ideal location for a small-scale holiday tree

This area of the layout is open for setting miniature Christmas village structures or placing wrapped presents.

A short train can orbit around the tree if an abundance of gifts obstructs the oval main line.

Holiday Village Railway

This traditional under-the-tree display is little more than a simple oval with a secondary loop. However, the arrangement makes an ideal setup for displaying a holiday tree, structures, and an operating toy train, which can make an appearance on two different routes.

The small circle of track provides a great place to position a Christmas tree, leaving the remaining oval loop open to display Christmas village structures, along with colorfully wrapped presents, of course!

When the tree comes down, the layout can remain operational, if you like. The village and scenery can stay relevant simply by adding simulated snow-capped mountains. You can form the mountains by carving then out of foam insulation board.

By Kent Johnson

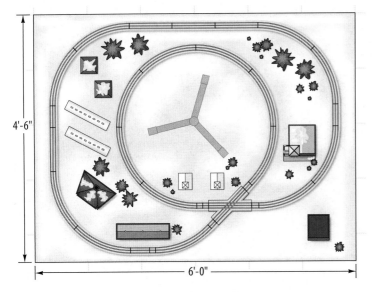

4'-6"

6'-0"

LIONEL FASTRACK COMPONENTS

Quantity	Description/Number
3	1.375 fitter
3	1.75-inch straight
1	4.5-inch straight
2	5-inch straight
4	10-inch straight
16	0-36 curve
1	45-degree crossing

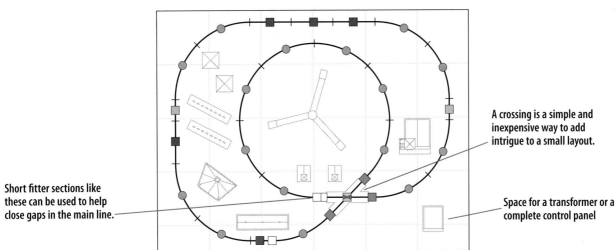

A crossing is a simple and inexpensive way to add intrigue to a small layout.

Short fitter sections like these can be used to help close gaps in the main line.

Space for a transformer or a complete control panel

Folded Figure Eight

When I learned our grand-daughter was visiting my wife Diana and me for Christmas, I was determined to make the holiday extra special by building an O gauge Christmas train layout.

I adapted a traditional tubular track folded figure-eight track plan from the December 2010 issue of *Classic Toy Trains*.

Earlier in the year, I had purchased a Lionel 30161 Boy Scouts of America train set and a 30069 Thomas and Friends set. Both sets included an oval of Lionel Fas-Track, and between them, I figured I could just about build the folded figure eight. I knew I had to purchase a

45-degree crossing and some 5-inch straights, and I guessed I could probably assemble the plan's custom-cut 3½-inch section by combining short sections of FasTrack.

From setback to success
The original plan fit in a 4 x 6-foot space, so I cut a piece of plywood to those dimensions and started to place track. It was at this point that I realized my Fas-Track curves were O-36, while the original plan had O-31 curves. Consequently, my track didn't fit on the table and it didn't go together like the diagram. [Now, this track plan could be completed using the new O-31 FasTrack curves.]

After giving the matter some thought, I figured my table had to be 4½ x 6 feet. Also, I would need FasTrack fitter sections of varying lengths to complete the plan.

I made a trip to my local hobby shop and purchased two or three of every short section I could find, so I could try out different track arrangements when I returned home.

After some trial and error, I finally built the FasTrack folded figure eight shown in the track plan and added the Christmas tree.

Witnessing the excitement of our granddaughter, nieces, and nephews enjoying the trains made it all worthwhile. We can't wait for next year!

By James Lowell Fry

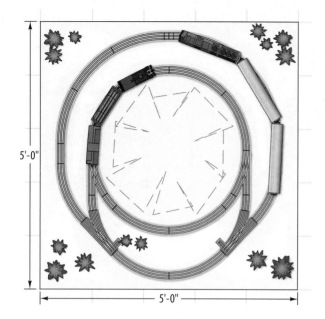

5'-0"

5'-0"

LIONEL FASTRACK COMPONENTS	
Quantity	Description/Number
2	1.375-inch straight (12073)
2	4.5-inch straight (12025)
10	O-36 curve, 45-degree (12015)
4	O-36 curve, 11.25-degree (12023)
6	O-48 curve, 30-degree (12043)
2	O-36 left-hand track switch, manual (12017)
2	O-36 right-hand track switch, manual (12018)

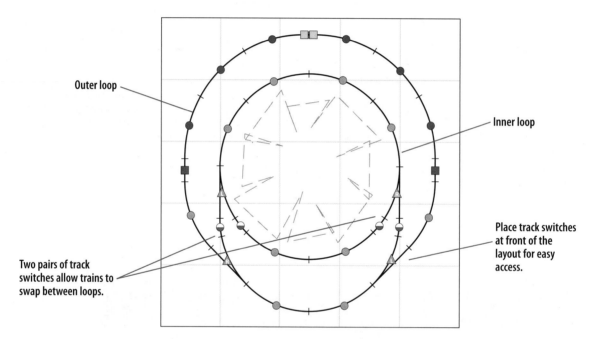

Outer loop

Inner loop

Two pairs of track switches allow trains to swap between loops.

Place track switches at front of the layout for easy access.

Slim Line Route

Every Christmas, my wife entrusts me to uphold exactly two holiday traditions. I'm charged with toting our artificial tree up from the basement and setting up a toy train display beneath the boughs. Thanks to some assistance from my son, I'm generally able to complete both tasks without much of an issue.

My wife loves to hang ornaments from the same long boughs that happen to

block the view of our toy train display. Short of purchasing an anemic Charlie Brown stick tree, I wondered if there might be an option that made allowances for both interests.

It seemed that a slim profile artificial tree was the perfect solution. These narrow, column-shaped trees feature boughs that can be less than half the length of a regular full tree. After setting up the tree, there was a place for ornaments, and the

train display was only partially obstructed.

To make the most of this unfettered area for trains, I designed a track plan that went a bit beyond a basic oval. In fact, two loops of Lionel FasTrack form a display pike in a 5-foot span, about the same space that a full-size tree occupies. The track switches at the front of the layout allow you to easily swap trains between the loops.

By Kent Johnson

Readers' Choice Urban Extension

s with most layouts, the *Classic Toy Trains'* Readers' Choice Railroad was an ongoing project. Designed with input from a survey of magazine readers, the building of the O gauge layout was featured in four 2011 issues (February, March, May, and July).

I developed the track plan for the 4 x 8-foot layout, which was built using traditional tubular track. The layout's setting was a mountainous area of the eastern United States, such as in the Appalachians. Along with that theme, readers desired realistic scenery more than a traditional toy train scenery treatment. There was also a preference for modern operating accessories.

Expanding the railroad

Later, the CTT staff decided to expand the railroad based on additional information from the readers' survey. As a number of readers wanted to see a layout featuring urban scenery, a 3 x 8-foot extension was added.

As you can imagine, pairing an Appalachian-themed railroad with big city lights and action might pose a challenge. But by culling all the hustle and bustle down to a few key elements, we managed to do precisely that.

Multistory office buildings, a constant blur of roadway traffic, a couple of large industries, and a feisty regional railroad that refuses to let a few cars and trucks get in the way all combined to form the urban scene.

Although the illuminated structures, operating vehicles, and various operating accessories keep the town buzzing, there was still enough Appalachian tree-lined terrain to suggest that quieter parts of the region lay over the mountain ridges.

Nonstop action

By using a SuperStreets starter set to form an independent loop for a bus or trolley, the action on this extension is virtually nonstop. The constantly moving roadway traffic, an operating factory accessory, and several illuminated structures, signs, and signals, and the CTTX railroad all contribute to the buzz about town.

When there isn't a CTTX coal train rolling down Main Street, the spring water bottling plant uses a versatile Lionel Trackmobile or a Ready Made Toys Beep locomotive to parade boxcars and tank cars between the main line and a pair of single car-length industrial spurs.

4'-0"

8'-0"

3'-0"

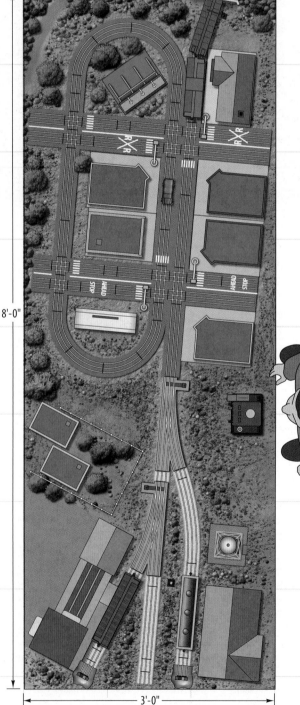

Maybe it's hard to imagine that a 24-square-foot layout or extension can actually accommodate all the activity and entertainment described here.

Adding the extension

The Readers' Choice Railroad extension used FasTrack components throughout and SuperStreets roadway sections to route along a street shared by automated vehicular traffic. While traditional tubular track was the resounding CTT reader favorite for the original layout, FasTrack was a popular alternative, so I redesigned the original layout's track plan using FasTrack, as described in pages 5–9.

When adding the expansion to the original layout, a full-scale (1" = 1") paper template was used to help align track and place structures. A downloadable version of this template is available at ctt.trains.com/operating/how to/2011/05/readers choice template.

This 3 x 8 urban extension can be added to a existing layout or, with all its entertaining action, it can be modified into a small stand-alone layout.

By Kent Johnson

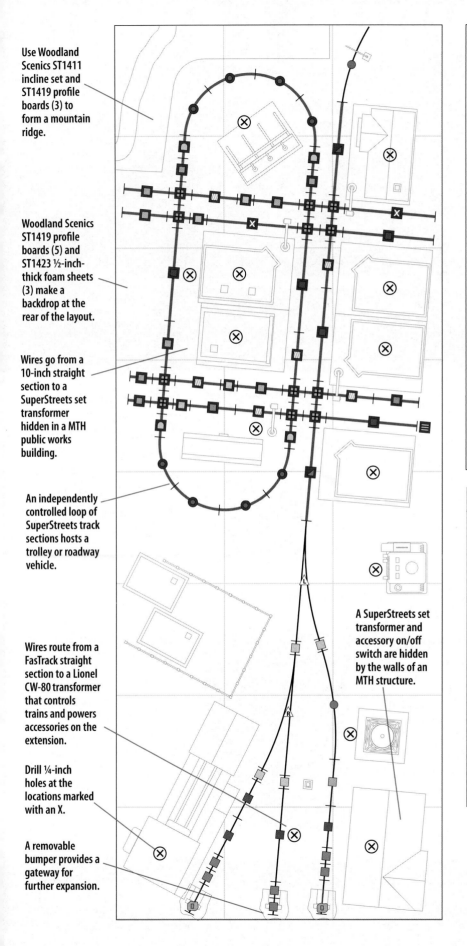

Use Woodland Scenics ST1411 incline set and ST1419 profile boards (3) to form a mountain ridge.

Woodland Scenics ST1419 profile boards (5) and ST1423 ½-inch-thick foam sheets (3) make a backdrop at the rear of the layout.

Wires go from a 10-inch straight section to a SuperStreets set transformer hidden in a MTH public works building.

An independently controlled loop of SuperStreets track sections hosts a trolley or roadway vehicle.

Wires route from a FasTrack straight section to a Lionel CW-80 transformer that controls trains and powers accessories on the extension.

Drill ¼-inch holes at the locations marked with an X.

A removable bumper provides a gateway for further expansion.

A SuperStreets set transformer and accessory on/off switch are hidden by the walls of an MTH structure.

LIONEL SUPERSTREETS

Quantity		Description/Number
4		2.5-inch straight, straight-to-curve (21261)
4		2.5-inch straight, straight-to-straight (22566)
5		5-inch straight (21433)
2		5-inch straight, stop ahead (21573)
6		5-inch straight, crosswalk (21574)
5		10-inch straight (21431)
2		10-inch straight, railroad crossing (21575)
1		10-inch transition, FasTrack (21164)
1		10-inch transition, O gauge (21284)
4		adjustable straight (22598)
8		D16 curve (21430)
12		intersection (21286)
1		barricade (22379)

LIONEL FASTRACK COMPONENTS

Quantity		Description/Number
4		1.375-inch straight (12074)
6		1.75-inch straight (12026)
3		4.5-inch straight (12025)
1		5-inch straight (12024)
1		10-inch straight (12014)
1		0-31 curve, 45-degree (37103)
1		0-60 curve, 22.5 degree (12056)
1		0-60 left-hand track switch (12057)
1		0-60 right-hand track switch (12058)
2		earthen bumper (12059)

SUGGESTED ACCESSORIES

Lionel

Number	Product
21390	Diner

MTH

Number	Product
30-9012	Corner drug store
30-9110	Operating transfer dock
30-11038	Modern dwarf signal
30-90007	Public works building
30-90019	Lombardi's Pizza
30-90032	Fairview depot
30-90069	Lenny's bagel shop
30-90159	PRR ticket office
30-90232	Owen Cash pawnshop
30-90239	Town house no. 2 (2)
30-90287	Lighted billboard
30-90291	Industrial water tower

BRING YOUR LAYOUT

TO LIFE!

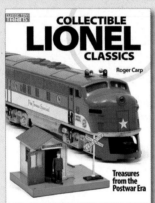

Collectible Lionel Classics

Get detailed information on 100 popular postwar Lionel locomotives, motorized units, rolling stock, and accessories! A description includes its history, common variations, and buying advice.

#10-8806 • $25.99

Greenberg's Repair and Operating Manual for Lionel Trains: 1945-1969

Find over a thousand repair and maintenance tips for Lionel locomotives, operating cars, accessories, transformers, light bulbs, switches, and more.

#10-8160 • $24.95

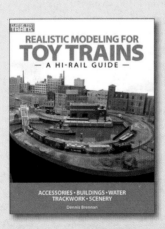

Realistic Modeling for Toy Trains

See step-by-step how various creative elements of a layout fit together. Practical building techniques and realistic modeling concepts explain how you can build a hi-rail toy train layout.

#10-8390 • $19.95

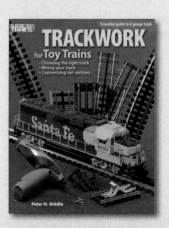

Trackwork for Toy Trains

Get an overview of the various lines of sectional and flexible track with step-by-step photography of the basic techniques for cutting, bending, wiring, and layout installation.

#10-8365 • $19.95

Kalmbach Media

Buy now from your local hobby shop!
Shop at KalmbachHobbyStore.com

Sales tax where applicable.